HUMAN BODY FACTORY

A GUIDE TO YOUR INSIDES

KINGFISHER
LONDON & NEW YORK

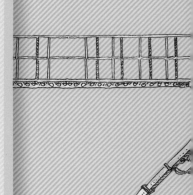

Text copyright © Macmillan Publishers
International Ltd. 2012, 2021, 2023
Illustrations copyright © Edmond Davis 2012, 2021, 2023
First published in 2012 in the United States by Kingfisher
This edition published in 2023 by Kingfisher
120 Broadway, New York, NY 10271
Kingfisher is an imprint of Macmillan Children's Books, London

Distributed in the U.S. and Canada by Macmillan,
120 Broadway, New York, NY 10271

Library of Congress Cataloging-in-Publication
data has been applied for.

Written by Dan Green and Catherine Brereton
Designed by Jake Da'Costa @ Intrepid Books Ltd.
Consultant: Dr. Patricia Macnair

ISBN 978-0-7534-7896-7

Kingfisher books are available for
special prootions and premiums.
For details contact: Special Markets Department,
Macmillan,120 Broadway, New York, NY 10271.

For more information, please visit www.kingfisherbooks.com

Printed in China
9 8 7 6 5 4 3 2 1
1TR/0323/WKT/UG/128MA

EU representative: 1st Floor, The Liffey Trust Centre,
117-126 Sheriff Street Upper, Dublin 1 D01 YC43

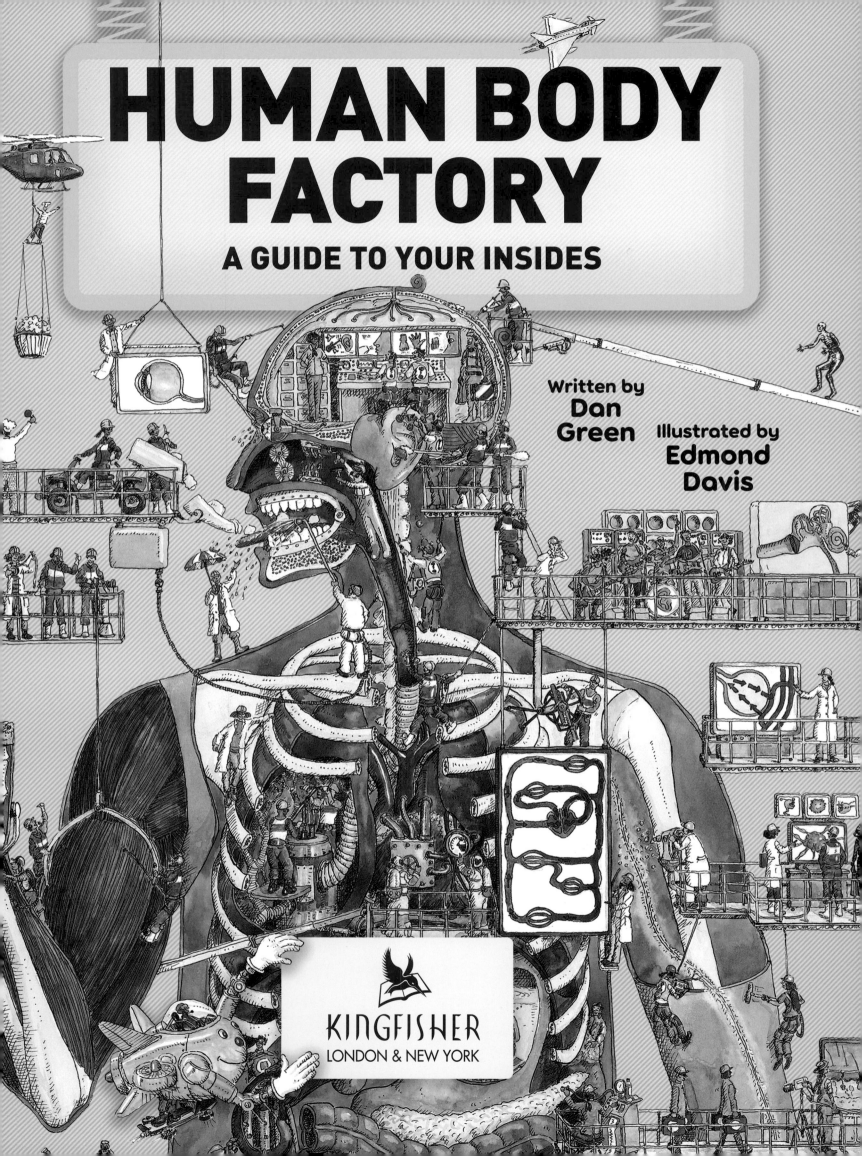

HUMAN BODY FACTORY

A GUIDE TO YOUR INSIDES

Written by
Dan Green

Illustrated by
Edmond Davis

KINGFISHER
LONDON & NEW YORK

CONTENTS

6-7 Introduction

8–9 Body Departments

10–11 The Brain

12–13 Eyes

14–15 Ears

16–17 Nose

18–19 Mouth

20-21 Hormones

22–23 Skin, Hair, and Nails

24–25 Heart

26–27 Blood

28–29 Immune System

30–31 Bones and Joints

32–33 Muscles

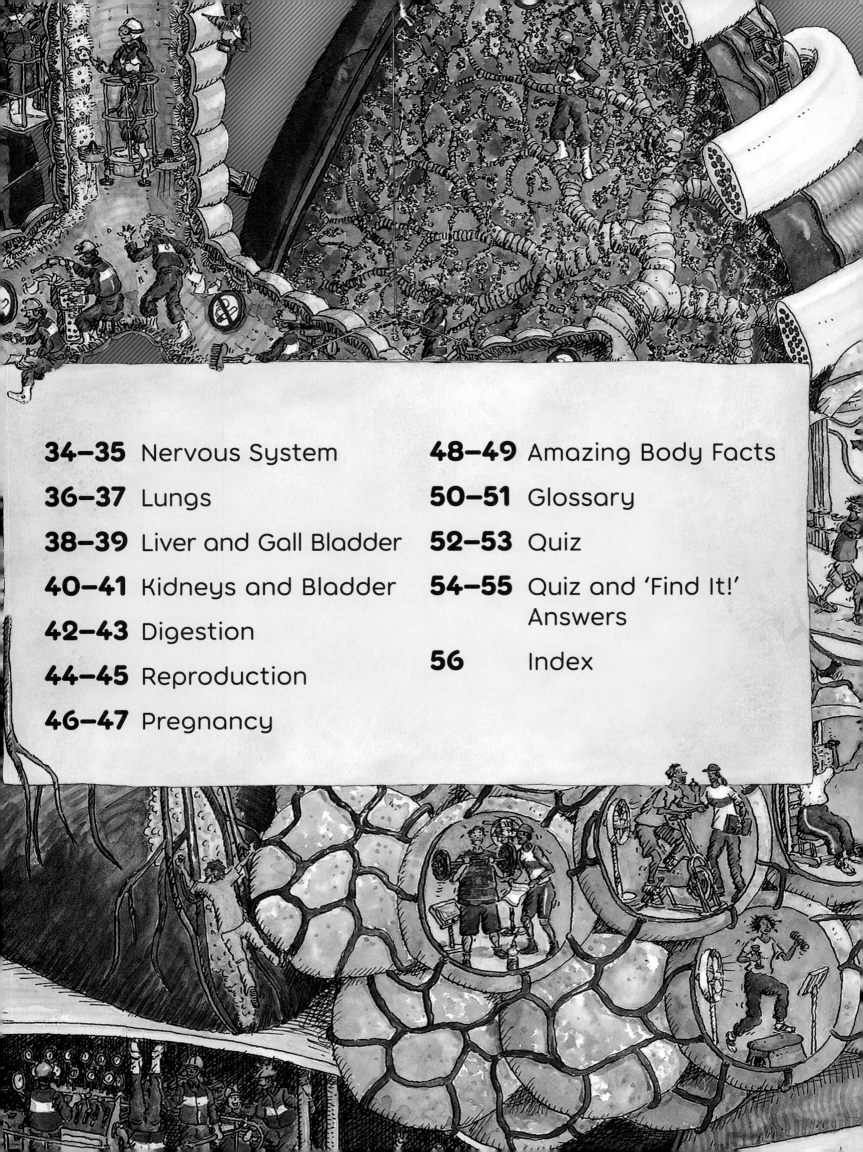

34–35 Nervous System

36–37 Lungs

38–39 Liver and Gall Bladder

40–41 Kidneys and Bladder

42–43 Digestion

44–45 Reproduction

46–47 Pregnancy

48–49 Amazing Body Facts

50–51 Glossary

52–53 Quiz

54–55 Quiz and 'Find It!' Answers

56 Index

HUMAN BODY FACTORY!

To check where you are in the body, look for the white dot on a figure like this.

YOU ARE HERE

The **brain** is the head office, and it's in charge. It coordinates everything in the body.

The **organs** are parts of the body that do a particular job. They include the lungs, heart, stomach, kidneys, brain, and many more.

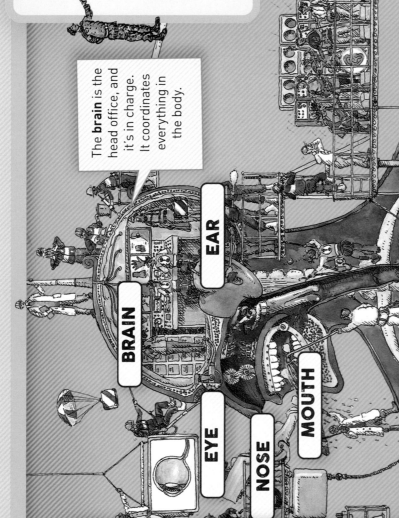

BRAIN

EAR

EYE

NOSE

MOUTH

HEART

STOMACH

SKELETON

Welcome to the Human Body Factory! You're about to burst through the doors of a bustling industrial plant, packed from head to toe with busy departments. You'll see inside your body as if it's a busy factory, teeming with wacky workers and marvelous machines. You'll discover the many different organs and body systems that keep the body functioning and buzzing with life.

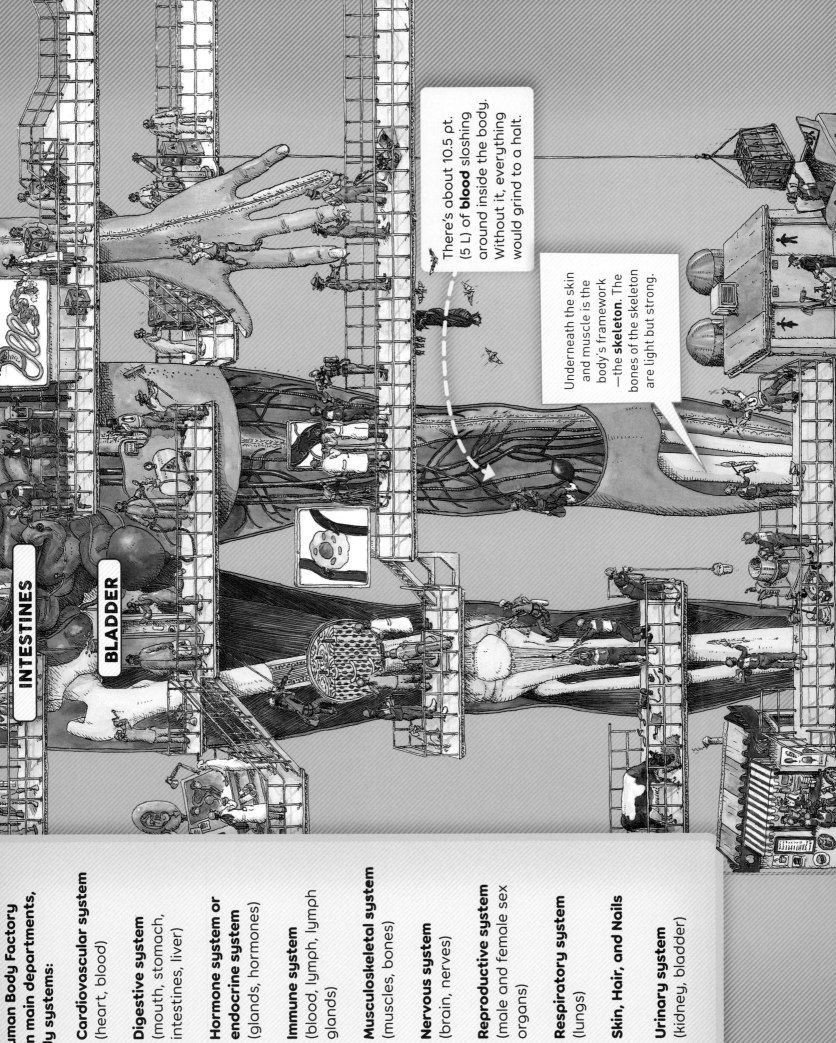

INTESTINES

BLADDER

There's about 10.5 pt. (5 L) of **blood** sloshing around inside the body. Without it, everything would grind to a halt.

Underneath the skin and muscle is the body's framework —the **skeleton**. The bones of the skeleton are light but strong.

The Human Body Factory has ten main departments, or body systems:

⚙ **Cardiovascular system** (heart, blood)

⚙ **Digestive system** (mouth, stomach, intestines, liver)

⚙ **Hormone system or endocrine system** (glands, hormones)

⚙ **Immune system** (blood, lymph, lymph glands)

⚙ **Musculoskeletal system** (muscles, bones)

⚙ **Nervous system** (brain, nerves)

⚙ **Reproductive system** (male and female sex organs)

⚙ **Respiratory system** (lungs)

⚙ **Skin, Hair, and Nails**

⚙ **Urinary system** (kidney, bladder)

BODY DEPARTMENTS

It's time for your Human Body Factory tour! You're about to take a wild roller-coaster ride around the cranking, sloshing, pumping parts that keep you alive and kicking! The departments are working nonstop to do their jobs, and there's no chance of a vacation around here! But how do they team up and work together? Here's a preview of what you'll be exploring . . .

The **respiratory system** draws oxygen into the body and gets rid of carbon dioxide. As you breathe in, air shoots in through the mouth or nose and goes to the lungs. The lungs pass the oxygen over to the blood and get carbon dioxide in return. Air shoots out again as you breathe out.

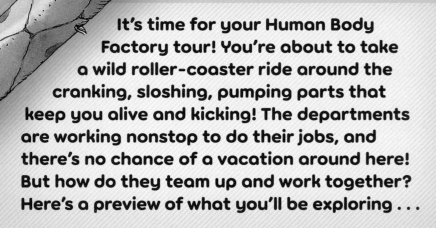

The different departments run along in their own ways, but they all need each other to keep the body healthy. They come together in the **ten major body systems**.

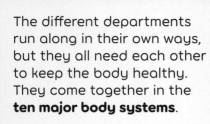

The **immune system** keeps the Human Body Factory healthy, using disease-killing cells. It's given a helping hand by the **skin, hair, and nails**, which wrap the body in a protective casing. Meanwhile, the **hormone system or endocrine system** monitors how body cells work and change, affecting how fast we burn energy and how we grow and develop.

As you go through the book, you'll see Body Factory workers doing all kinds of things. Look out for a skeleton and sometimes a vampire joining in the activities!

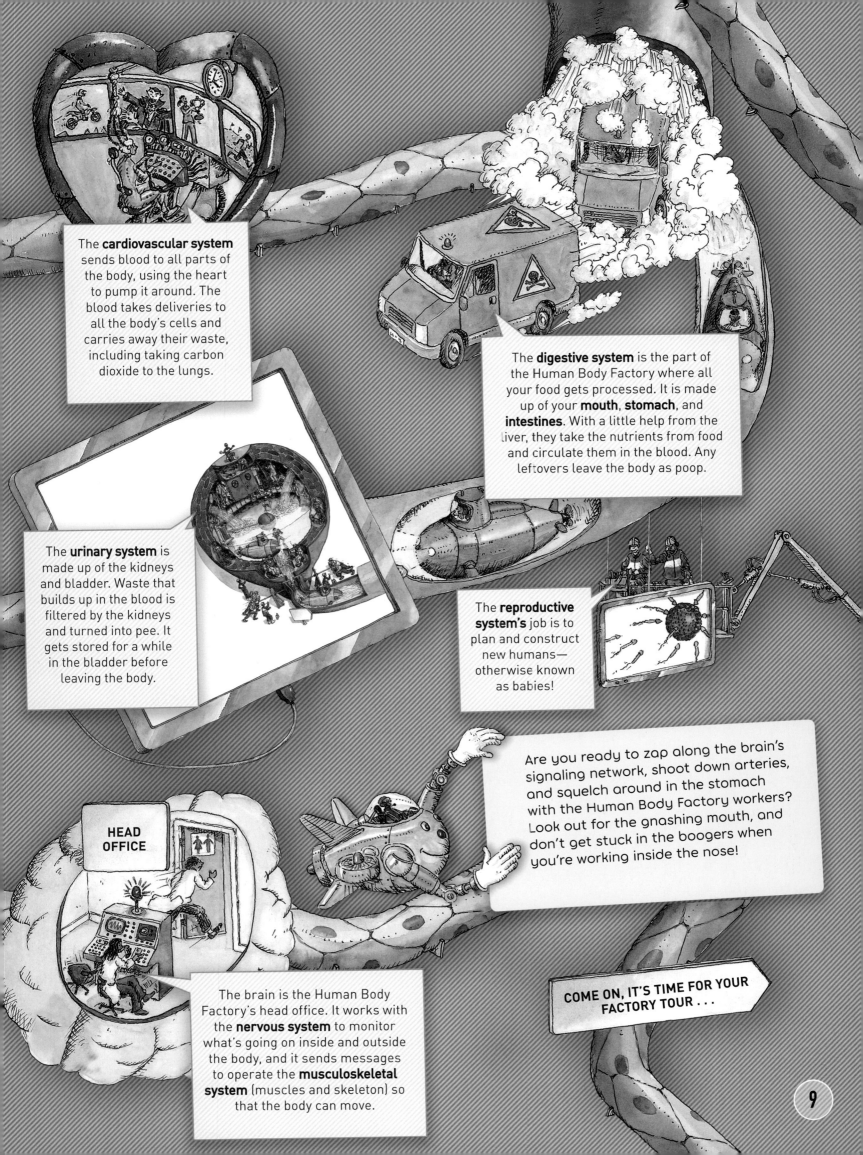

The **cardiovascular system** sends blood to all parts of the body, using the heart to pump it around. The blood takes deliveries to all the body's cells and carries away their waste, including taking carbon dioxide to the lungs.

The **digestive system** is the part of the Human Body Factory where all your food gets processed. It is made up of your **mouth**, **stomach**, and **intestines**. With a little help from the liver, they take the nutrients from food and circulate them in the blood. Any leftovers leave the body as poop.

The **urinary system** is made up of the kidneys and bladder. Waste that builds up in the blood is filtered by the kidneys and turned into pee. It gets stored for a while in the bladder before leaving the body.

The **reproductive system's** job is to plan and construct new humans—otherwise known as babies!

Are you ready to zap along the brain's signaling network, shoot down arteries, and squelch around in the stomach with the Human Body Factory workers? Look out for the gnashing mouth, and don't get stuck in the boogers when you're working inside the nose!

HEAD OFFICE

The brain is the Human Body Factory's head office. It works with the **nervous system** to monitor what's going on inside and outside the body, and it sends messages to operate the **musculoskeletal system** (muscles and skeleton) so that the body can move.

COME ON, IT'S TIME FOR YOUR FACTORY TOUR . . .

THE BRAIN

Neurons are the cells that do a lot of the brainwork. Fibers link them all together in a vast, amazing, superfast network.

The Human Body Factory has a busy head office—the brain! This control center is in charge of bossing all the body's activities. It controls movements, generates thoughts, dreams, and memories, and is great at problem solving. It does all this brainy work using nerve cells called neurons, which zap signals around at lightning speed.

The **thalamus** carries movement and sense signals to the correct parts of the brain.

The **hippocampus** makes and stores memories.

YOU ARE HERE

The **hypothalamus** works closely with the endocrine system (see pages 20–21).

OWNER'S MANUAL:
Meet your brain

 How heavy? approx. 3 lb. (1.4 kg)

 How much energy? makes up 20 percent of the body's energy usage

 Number of neurons: approx. 86 billion

 Neuron length: up to 3 ft. (1 m)—the longest cells in the body!

Blood vessels supply the brain with LOTS of energy and oxygen.

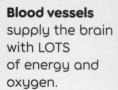

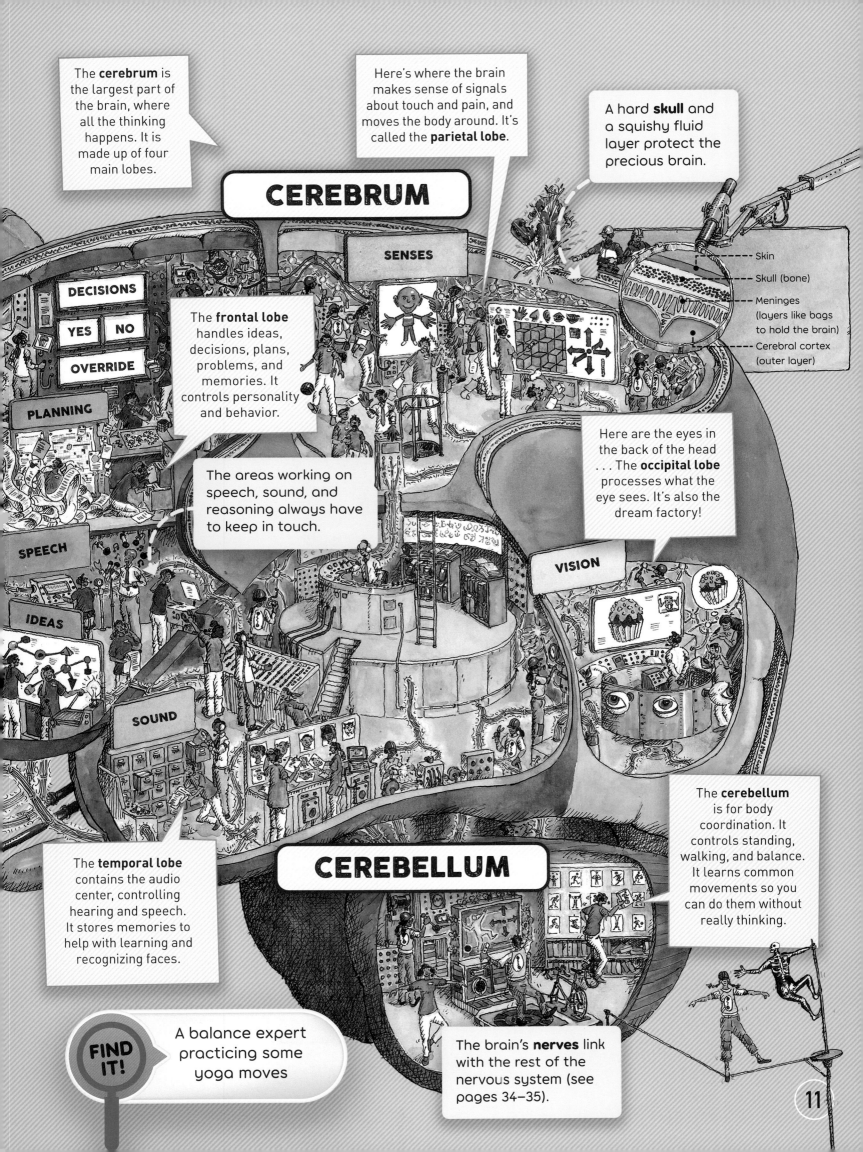

EYES

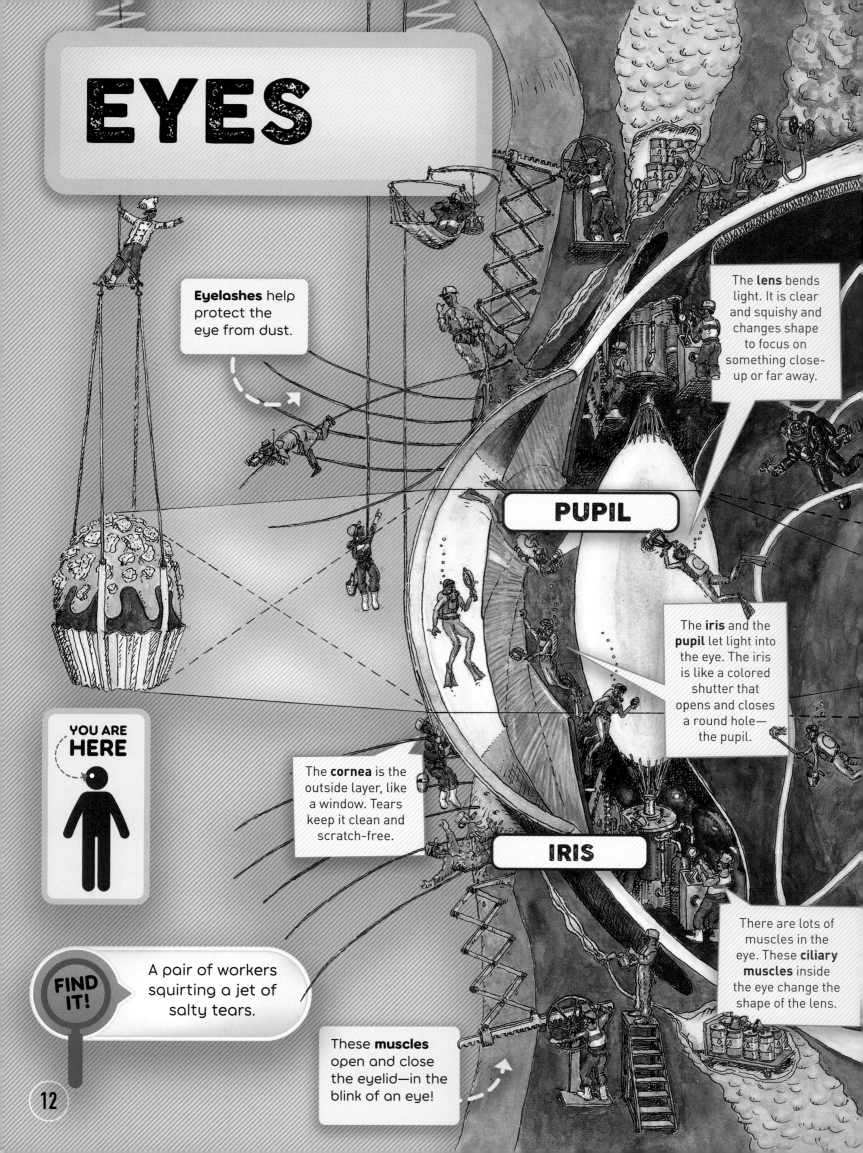

Eyelashes help protect the eye from dust.

The **lens** bends light. It is clear and squishy and changes shape to focus on something close-up or far away.

PUPIL

The **iris** and the **pupil** let light into the eye. The iris is like a colored shutter that opens and closes a round hole—the pupil.

YOU ARE **HERE**

The **cornea** is the outside layer, like a window. Tears keep it clean and scratch-free.

IRIS

There are lots of muscles in the eye. These **ciliary muscles** inside the eye change the shape of the lens.

FIND IT!

A pair of workers squirting a jet of salty tears.

These **muscles** open and close the eyelid—in the blink of an eye!

The eyes are the spy hubs of the Human Body Factory! They work like two cameras, taking in light and making pictures for the body to see. Lenses bend the light coming in and focus it onto light-sensing cells. These zap signals to the brain, which makes sense of all the pictures.

- **How many sense cells?** approx. 120 million rods and 6 million cones
- **How many colors?** the eye can see up to 10 million shades of color!
- **How many blinks?** approx. 10,000 a day
- **Fastest muscles:** the muscles that move the eye are the fastest in the body

e eye is full
gel called
reous humor.

The **brain** sends messages to the eye, telling the muscles to make precise movements to focus on that cupcake in view.

RETINA

The **retina** lines the back of the eye. It is packed with light-sensing cells. Light beaming into the eye hits the retina.

The **image** beamed onto the retina is upside down.

The light-sensing cells are called **rods and cones**. Rods are for low-light vision, and cones are for color vision.

OPTIC NERVE

The **optic nerve** zaps signals from the retina to the brain. It sends a huge amount of information at high speed.

The brain will sort the information, **turn it the right way up,** and make sense of it —so you can see the cupcake!

These **muscles** attached to the outside of the eye move the whole eye up and down and side to side.

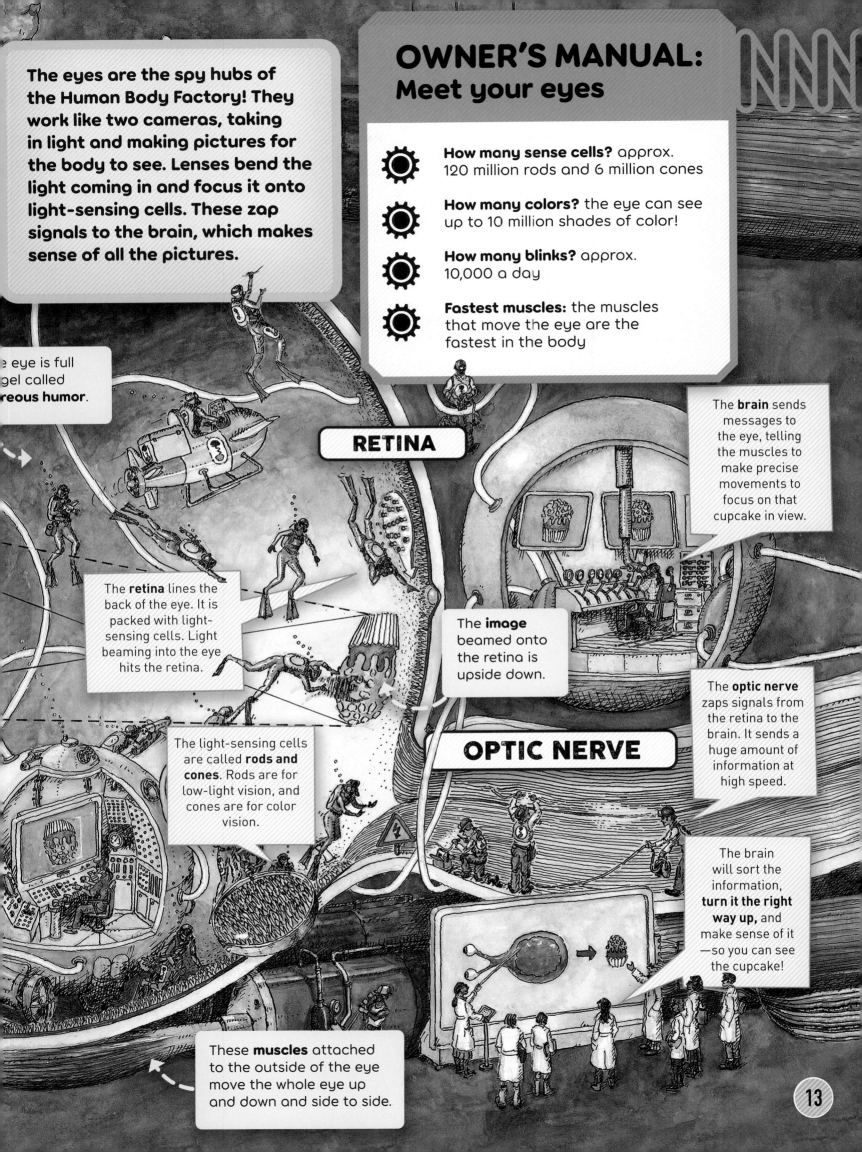

EARS

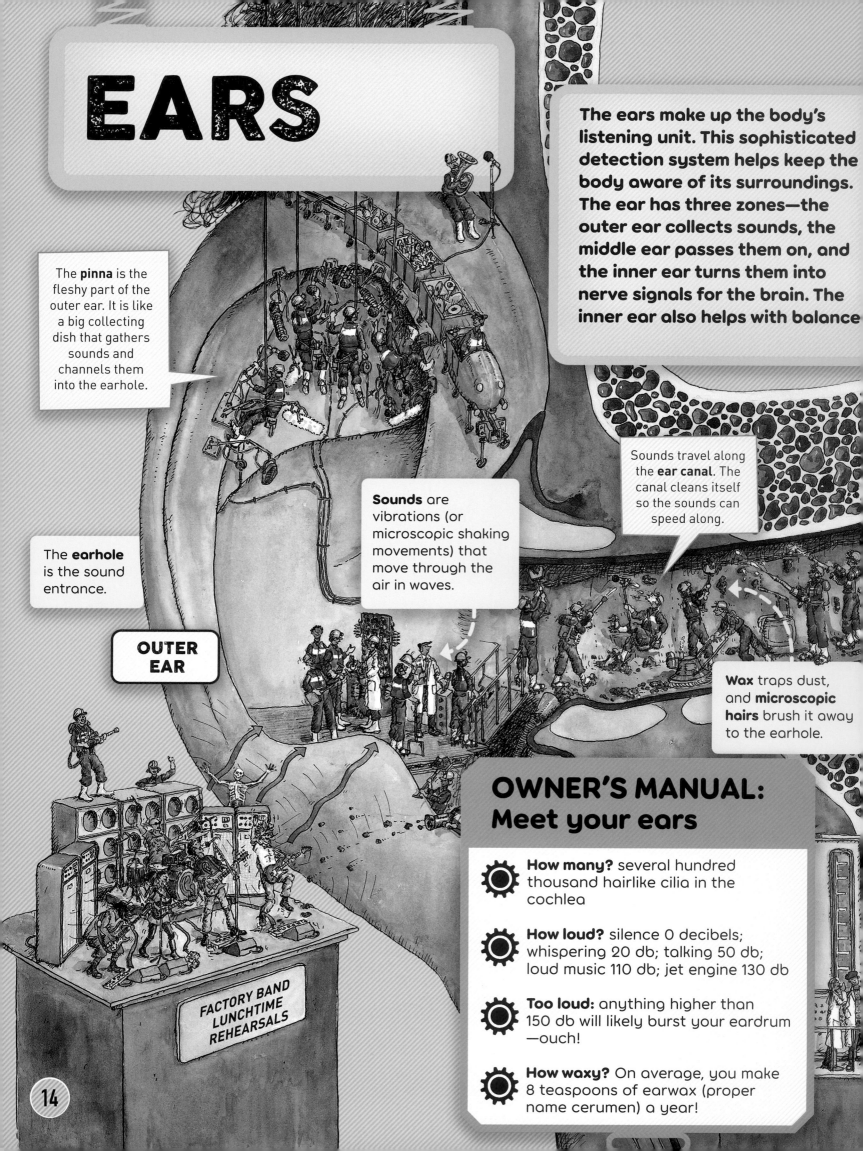

The ears make up the body's listening unit. This sophisticated detection system helps keep the body aware of its surroundings. The ear has three zones—the outer ear collects sounds, the middle ear passes them on, and the inner ear turns them into nerve signals for the brain. The inner ear also helps with balance

The **pinna** is the fleshy part of the outer ear. It is like a big collecting dish that gathers sounds and channels them into the earhole.

The **earhole** is the sound entrance.

OUTER EAR

Sounds are vibrations (or microscopic shaking movements) that move through the air in waves.

Sounds travel along the **ear canal**. The canal cleans itself so the sounds can speed along.

Wax traps dust, and **microscopic hairs** brush it away to the earhole.

FACTORY BAND LUNCHTIME REHEARSALS

OWNER'S MANUAL: Meet your ears

- **How many?** several hundred thousand hairlike cilia in the cochlea

- **How loud?** silence 0 decibels; whispering 20 db; talking 50 db; loud music 110 db; jet engine 130 db

- **Too loud:** anything higher than 150 db will likely burst your eardrum —ouch!

- **How waxy?** On average, you make 8 teaspoons of earwax (proper name cerumen) a year!

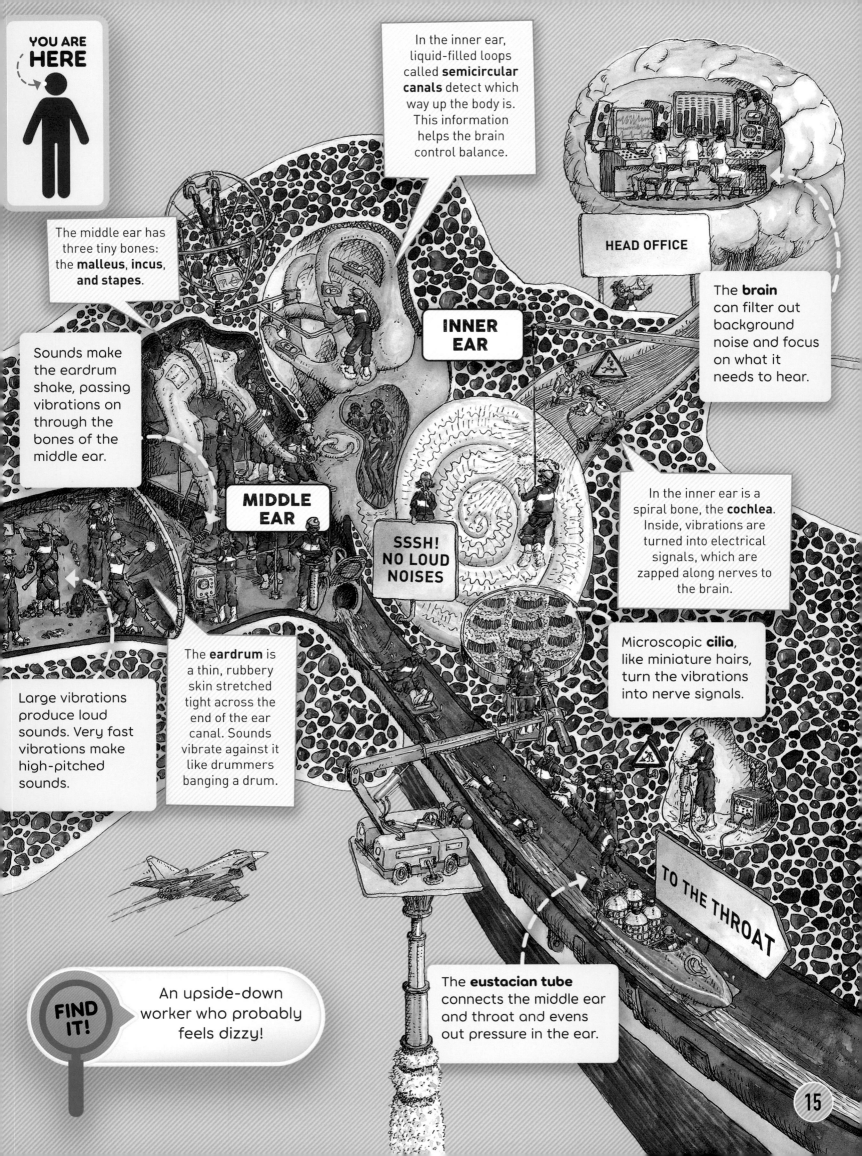

YOU ARE HERE

In the inner ear, liquid-filled loops called **semicircular canals** detect which way up the body is. This information helps the brain control balance.

HEAD OFFICE

The middle ear has three tiny bones: the **malleus**, **incus**, **and stapes**.

The **brain** can filter out background noise and focus on what it needs to hear.

Sounds make the eardrum shake, passing vibrations on through the bones of the middle ear.

INNER EAR

MIDDLE EAR

SSSH! NO LOUD NOISES

In the inner ear is a spiral bone, the **cochlea**. Inside, vibrations are turned into electrical signals, which are zapped along nerves to the brain.

Large vibrations produce loud sounds. Very fast vibrations make high-pitched sounds.

The **eardrum** is a thin, rubbery skin stretched tight across the end of the ear canal. Sounds vibrate against it like drummers banging a drum.

Microscopic **cilia**, like miniature hairs, turn the vibrations into nerve signals.

TO THE THROAT

FIND IT!

An upside-down worker who probably feels dizzy!

The **eustacian tube** connects the middle ear and throat and evens out pressure in the ear.

NOSE

The nose is the body's top chemical detection department. Deep inside it is a patch of nerve endings that sense smells, stenches, and aromas. And the nose has another job that's just as important. It moistens and cleans air on its way in to your lungs, stopping lots of unwanted stuff from getting in.

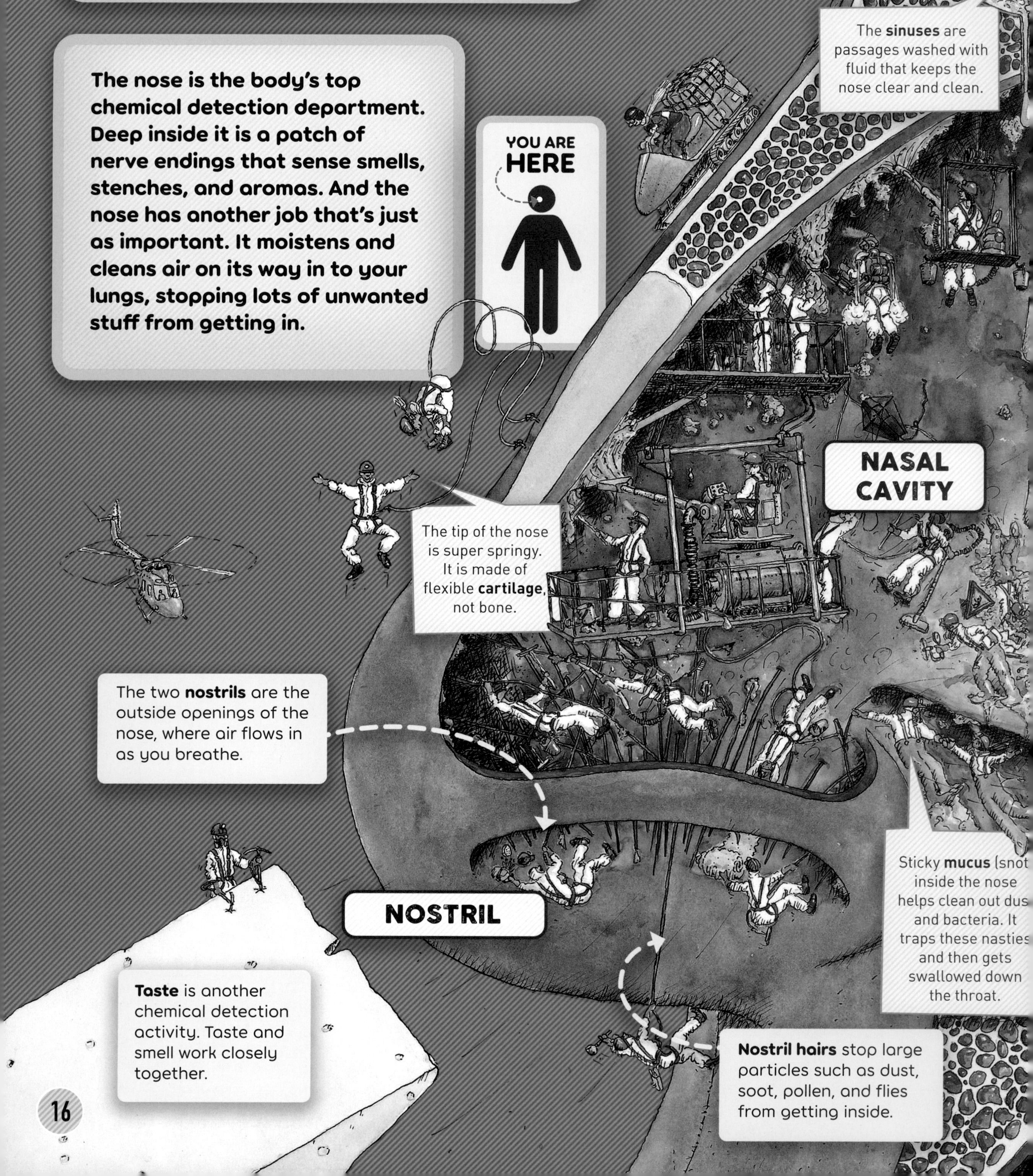

YOU ARE
HERE

SINUS

The **sinuses** are passages washed with fluid that keeps the nose clear and clean.

NASAL CAVITY

The tip of the nose is super springy. It is made of flexible **cartilage**, not bone.

The two **nostrils** are the outside openings of the nose, where air flows in as you breathe.

Sticky **mucus** (snot) inside the nose helps clean out dust and bacteria. It traps these nasties and then gets swallowed down the throat.

NOSTRIL

Taste is another chemical detection activity. Taste and smell work closely together.

Nostril hairs stop large particles such as dust, soot, pollen, and flies from getting inside.

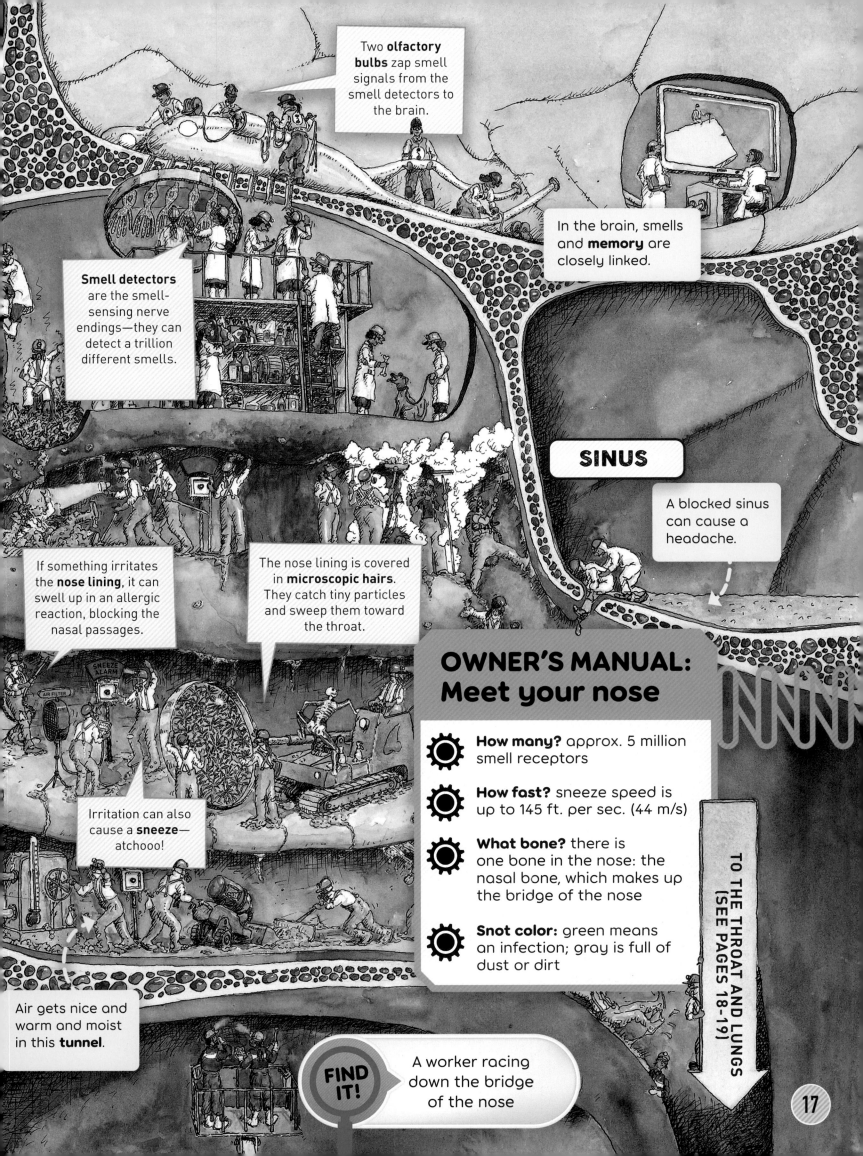

MOUTH

Soaking in slurpy saliva, the mouth has a lot going on. It is the entrance area to your digestive system, and it mashes up almost anything that comes in as it gulps, guzzles, and grinds. In come food and drink, and out go coughs, hiccups, and sometimes even—gross!—vomit.

Tonsils help block germs from entering the body and help the immune system (see pages 28–29).

There are 32 **teeth**, stuck into the bones of the skull. Pink, healthy gums hold them in place.

YOU ARE **HERE**

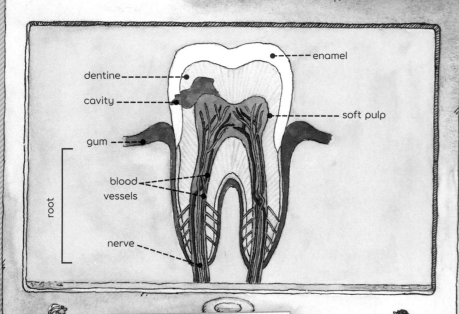

- enamel
- dentine
- cavity
- soft pulp
- gum
- blood vessels
- root
- nerve

Each tooth has a very hard outer layer called **enamel**, a hard layer called **dentine**, and a soft center where the **nerves** and **blood vessels** are found.

TONSIL

AIR

FOOD

A **flap** at the back of the throat stops food from going down the windpipe.

FIND IT! A saliva-gland diver taking a photo

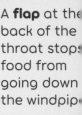

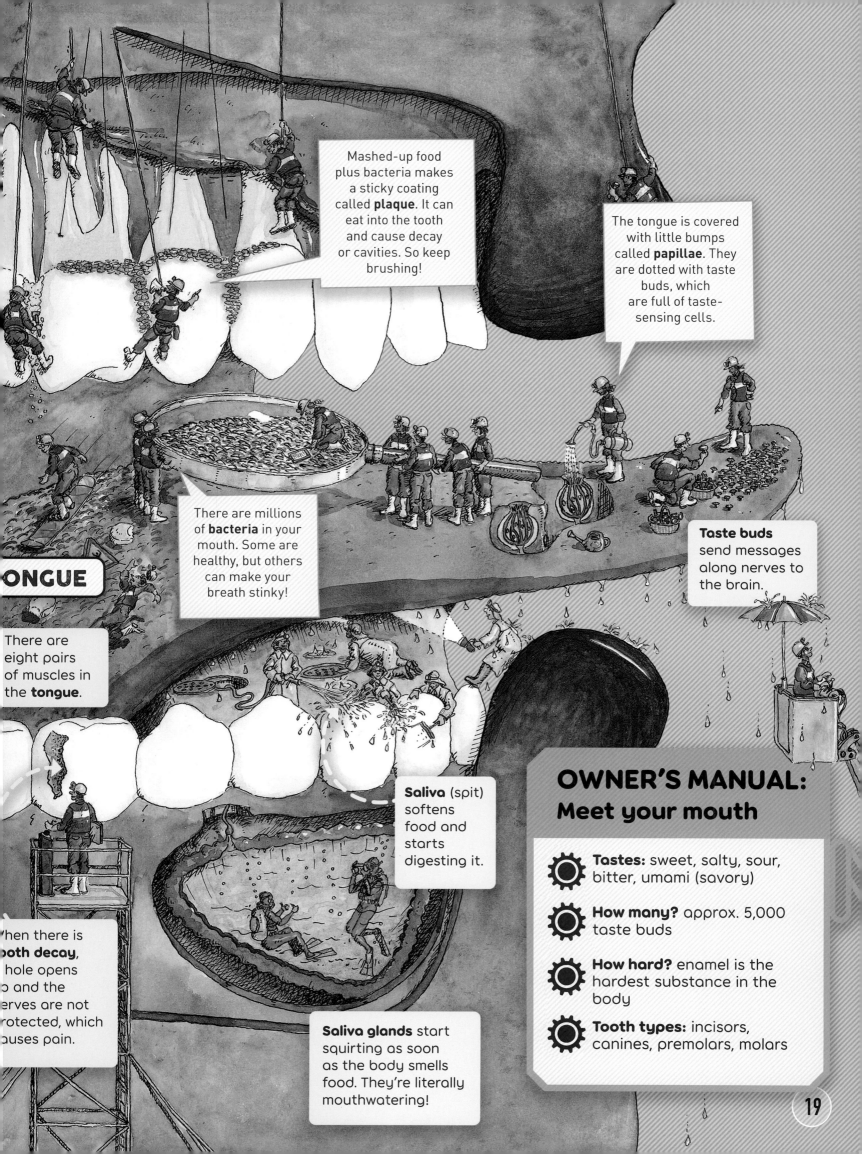

HORMONES

The body has a system of chemical messenger agents called hormones. They carry messages around the body to change the way cells operate and keep everything in balance. Hormones are made in glands and speed along the bloodstream to where they're needed. Working together, the whole system of hormone messenger agents is called the endocrine system.

The **pituitary gland** is the hormone control center. It sends lots of chemical messages to other glands telling them how much of each hormone they need to make.

The pituitary gland makes and sends some hormones of its own, including **growth hormone**.

When a person is stressed or doing a lot of exercise, the **adrenal gland** makes hormones that make the heart race and get the body ready for action.

The **thyroid gland** makes hormones that control how quickly body cells do their work and how much energy they burn.

Hormone messengers fe back informat so the glands keep things in balance.

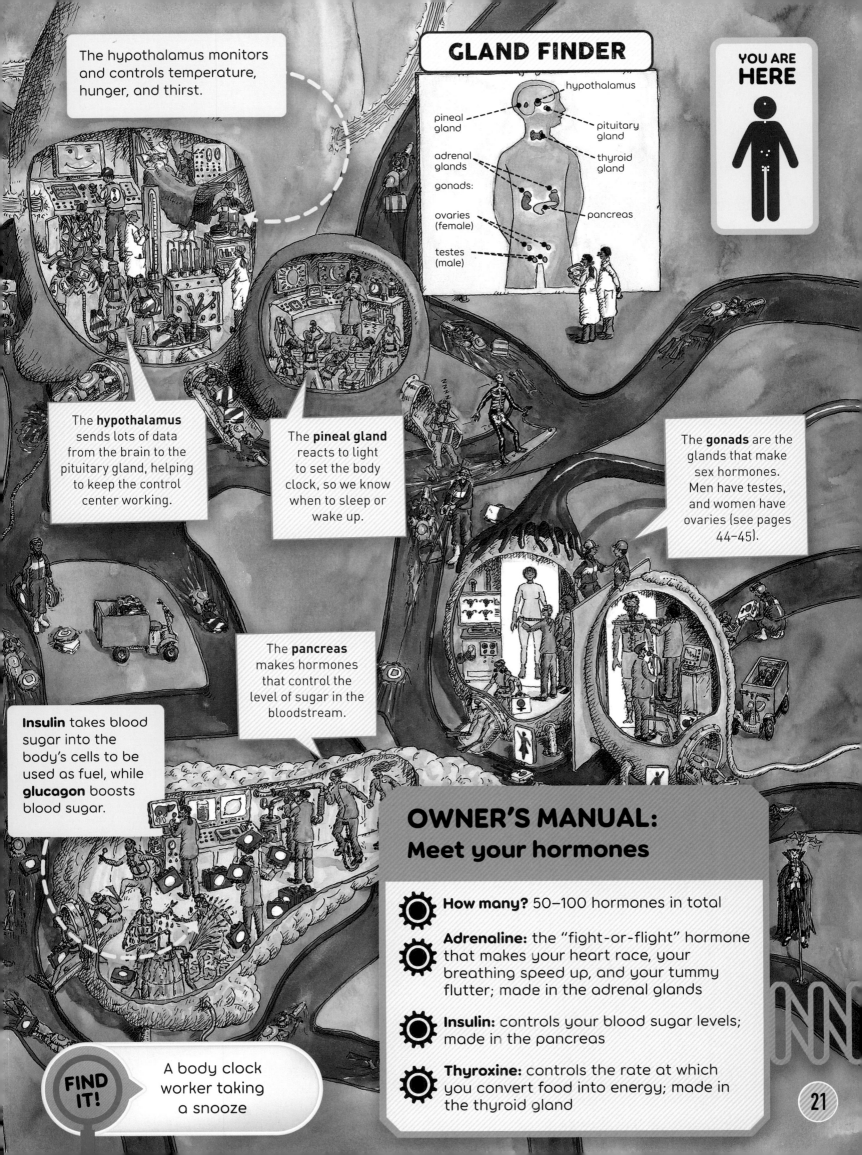

The hypothalamus monitors and controls temperature, hunger, and thirst.

GLAND FINDER

- hypothalamus
- pineal gland
- pituitary gland
- adrenal glands
- thyroid gland
- gonads:
- ovaries (female)
- pancreas
- testes (male)

YOU ARE **HERE**

The **hypothalamus** sends lots of data from the brain to the pituitary gland, helping to keep the control center working.

The **pineal gland** reacts to light to set the body clock, so we know when to sleep or wake up.

The **gonads** are the glands that make sex hormones. Men have testes, and women have ovaries (see pages 44–45).

The **pancreas** makes hormones that control the level of sugar in the bloodstream.

Insulin takes blood sugar into the body's cells to be used as fuel, while **glucagon** boosts blood sugar.

OWNER'S MANUAL:
Meet your hormones

⚙ **How many?** 50–100 hormones in total

⚙ **Adrenaline:** the "fight-or-flight" hormone that makes your heart race, your breathing speed up, and your tummy flutter; made in the adrenal glands

⚙ **Insulin:** controls your blood sugar levels; made in the pancreas

⚙ **Thyroxine:** controls the rate at which you convert food into energy; made in the thyroid gland

FIND IT! A body clock worker taking a snooze

21

SKIN, HAIR, AND NAILS

Skin is the body's first line of defense. It is made of a tough outer layer called the **epidermis**, a stretchy middle layer called the **dermis**, and a layer of spongy **fat**.

The **fingertips** are super sensitive. Special cells send messages to the brain so you know how hard or gently to grip things.

Nails protect the ends of the fingers. They're made from the same material as hair, only harder. They are also tools for scratching or picking up small things.

Every person's **fingerprints** are unique to them alone.

The dermis is packed with **sensors** that detect pain, heat, cold, pressure, and vibrations.

The Human Body Factory is wrapped in a high-tech superskin that keeps it cool and watertight and protects it from the world outside. The skin covers the whole body and is its largest organ. It is full of sensors allowing it to touch and feel the world, and it can even repair itself when it gets torn or broken.

YOU ARE HERE

DERMIS

The **fat layer** helps keep the body warm and acts like a protective cushion.

OWNER'S MANUAL:
Meet your skin, hair, and nails

⚙ **How big?** skin covers 22 sq. ft. (2 m²) and weighs 9 lb. (4 kg)

⚙ **How thick?** from 0.02 in. (0.5 mm) around the eyes to 0.2 in. (5 mm) on the soles of the feet

⚙ **How sweaty?** 3.5 pt. (1.7 L) of sweat produced on a hot day

⚙ **What color?** Melanin in the skin gives skin its color

Billions of **bacteria** live on the skin's surface and help fight really nasty germs.

The amount of blood flowing through tiny **blood vessels** near the surface helps keep the body cool or warm.

The skin keeps things cool by pumping **sweat** to the surface—the sweat evaporates, which cools the skin off.

EPIDERMIS

Nerves in the sensors send signals to the brain.

Sweat is made in **sweat glands** and spurts out of little holes called pores.

Oil glands make oil to keep the skin stretchy and watertight.

Each **hair** grows from a pit called a **follicle**. It has its own nerve fibers and a muscle that makes it stand up or lie flat.

FIND IT! Surface workers finding their own ways to cool down under hot lights

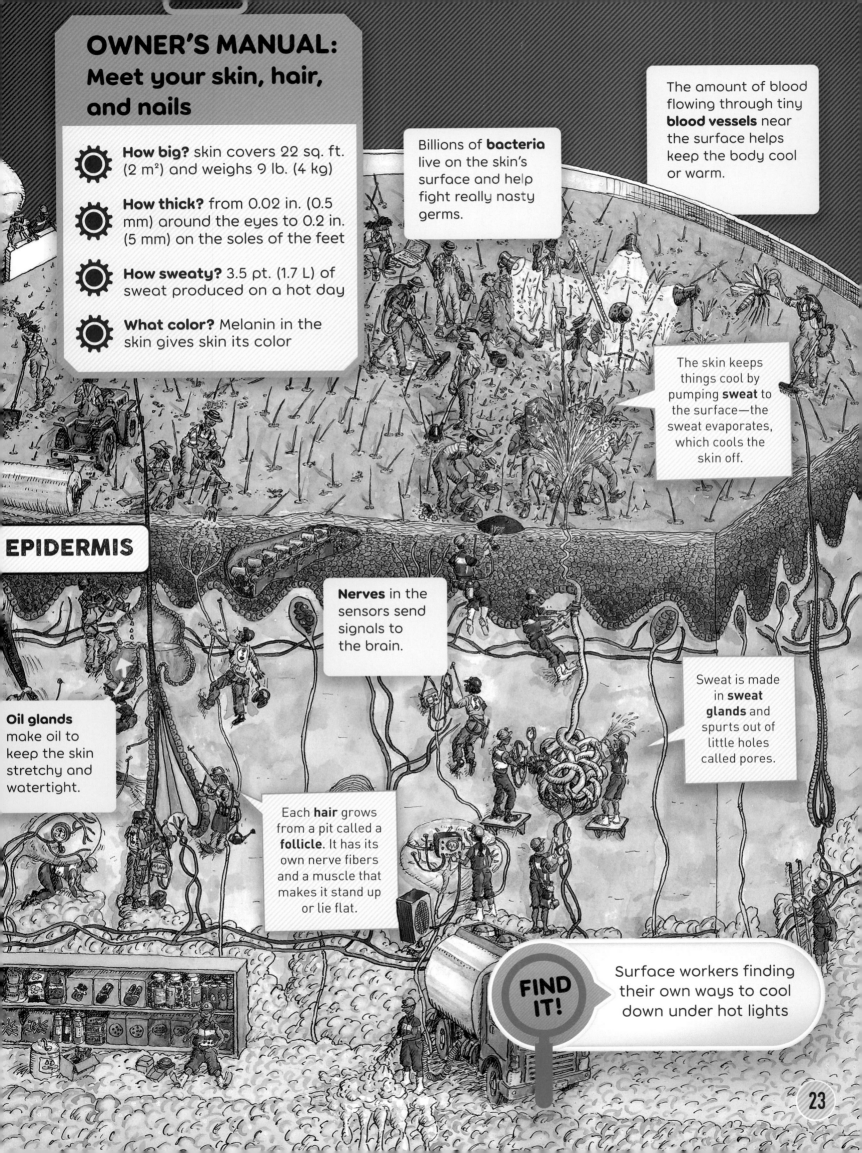

23

HEART

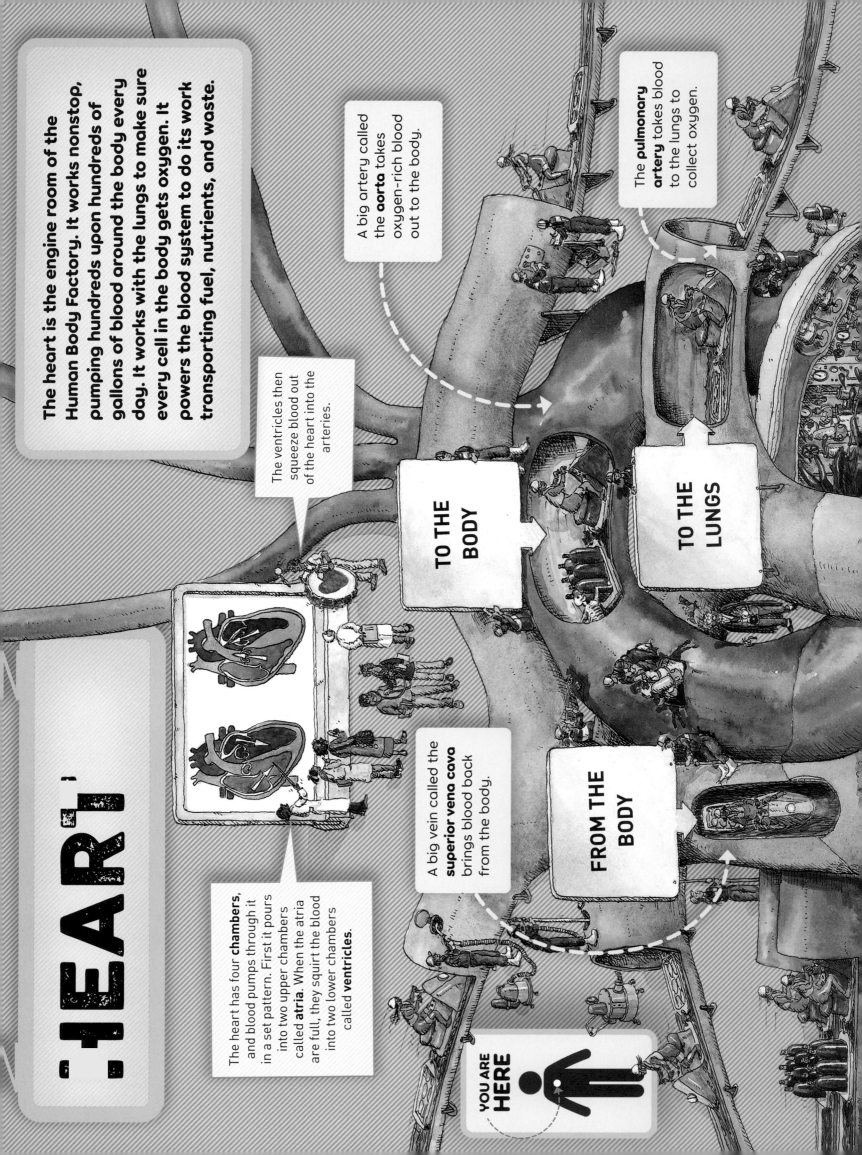

The heart is the engine room of the Human Body Factory. It works nonstop, pumping hundreds upon hundreds of gallons of blood around the body every day. It works with the lungs to make sure every cell in the body gets oxygen. It **powers the blood system to do its work** transporting fuel, nutrients, and waste.

The ventricles then squeeze blood out of the heart into the arteries.

The heart has four **chambers,** and blood pumps through it in a set pattern. First it pours into two upper chambers called **atria.** When the atria are full, they squirt the blood into two lower chambers called **ventricles.**

A big artery called the **aorta** takes oxygen-rich blood out to the body.

The **pulmonary artery** takes blood to the lungs to collect oxygen.

TO THE BODY

TO THE LUNGS

A big vein called the **superior vena cava** brings blood back from the body.

FROM THE BODY

YOU ARE **HERE**

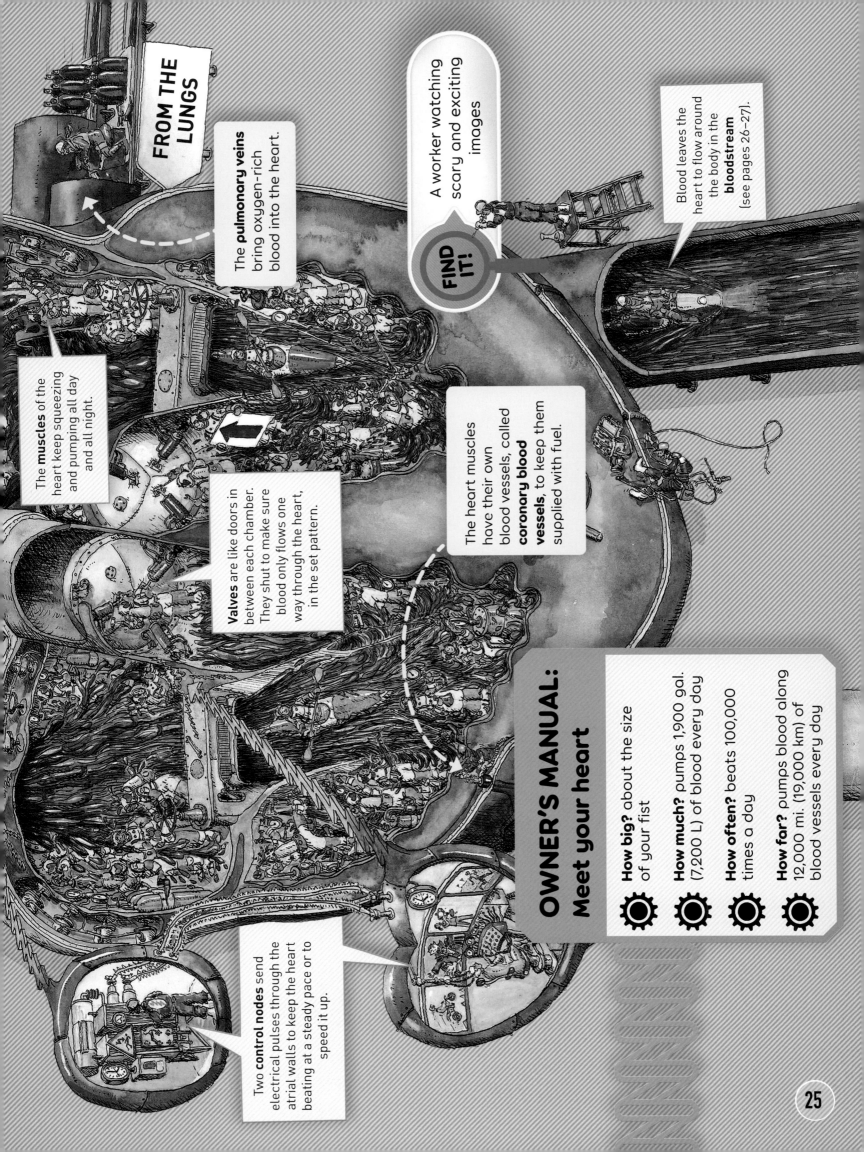

FROM THE LUNGS

The **pulmonary veins** bring oxygen-rich blood into the heart.

The **muscles** of the heart keep squeezing and pumping all day and all night.

Valves are like doors in between each chamber. They shut to make sure blood only flows one way through the heart, in the set pattern.

A worker watching scary and exciting images

FIND IT!

Blood leaves the heart to flow around the body in the **bloodstream** (see pages 26–27).

The heart muscles have their own blood vessels, called **coronary blood vessels**, to keep them supplied with fuel.

Two **control nodes** send electrical pulses through the atrial walls to keep the heart beating at a steady pace or to speed it up.

OWNER'S MANUAL: Meet your heart

⚙ **How big?** about the size of your fist

⚙ **How much?** pumps 1,900 gal. (7,200 L) of blood every day

⚙ **How often?** beats 100,000 times a day

⚙ **How far?** pumps blood along 12,000 mi. (19,000 km) of blood vessels every day

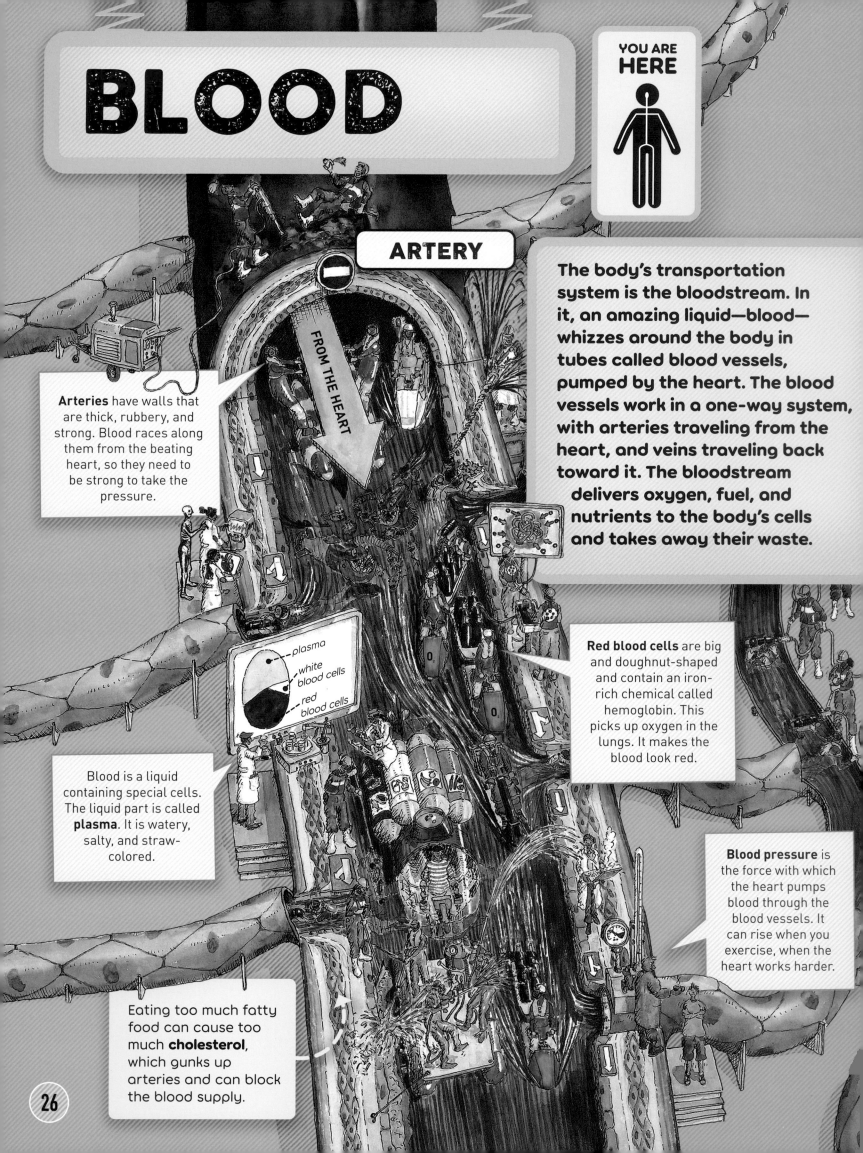

BLOOD

ARTERY

FROM THE HEART

The body's transportation system is the bloodstream. In it, an amazing liquid—blood—whizzes around the body in tubes called blood vessels, pumped by the heart. The blood vessels work in a one-way system, with arteries traveling from the heart, and veins traveling back toward it. The bloodstream delivers oxygen, fuel, and nutrients to the body's cells and takes away their waste.

Arteries have walls that are thick, rubbery, and strong. Blood races along them from the beating heart, so they need to be strong to take the pressure.

plasma

white blood cells

red blood cells

Blood is a liquid containing special cells. The liquid part is called **plasma**. It is watery, salty, and straw-colored.

Red blood cells are big and doughnut-shaped and contain an iron-rich chemical called hemoglobin. This picks up oxygen in the lungs. It makes the blood look red.

Blood pressure is the force with which the heart pumps blood through the blood vessels. It can rise when you exercise, when the heart works harder.

Eating too much fatty food can cause too much **cholesterol**, which gunks up arteries and can block the blood supply.

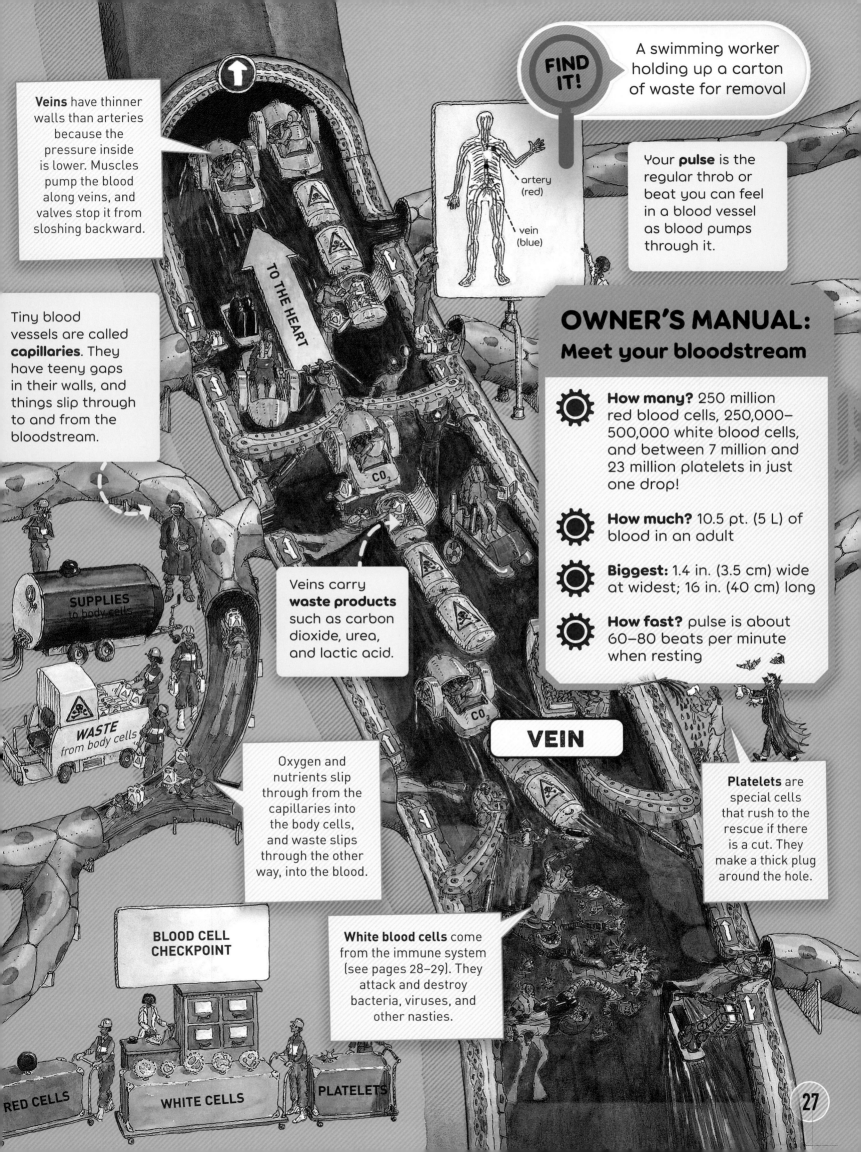

Veins have thinner walls than arteries because the pressure inside is lower. Muscles pump the blood along veins, and valves stop it from sloshing backward.

Tiny blood vessels are called **capillaries**. They have teeny gaps in their walls, and things slip through to and from the bloodstream.

TO THE HEART

SUPPLIES to body cells

WASTE from body cells

Veins carry **waste products** such as carbon dioxide, urea, and lactic acid.

Oxygen and nutrients slip through from the capillaries into the body cells, and waste slips through the other way, into the blood.

BLOOD CELL CHECKPOINT

RED CELLS   WHITE CELLS   PLATELETS

White blood cells come from the immune system (see pages 28–29). They attack and destroy bacteria, viruses, and other nasties.

FIND IT! A swimming worker holding up a carton of waste for removal

artery (red)

vein (blue)

Your **pulse** is the regular throb or beat you can feel in a blood vessel as blood pumps through it.

OWNER'S MANUAL:
Meet your bloodstream

⚙ **How many?** 250 million red blood cells, 250,000–500,000 white blood cells, and between 7 million and 23 million platelets in just one drop!

⚙ **How much?** 10.5 pt. (5 L) of blood in an adult

⚙ **Biggest:** 1.4 in. (3.5 cm) wide at widest; 16 in. (40 cm) long

⚙ **How fast?** pulse is about 60–80 beats per minute when resting

VEIN

Platelets are special cells that rush to the rescue if there is a cut. They make a thick plug around the hole.

IMMUNE SYSTEM

The body's emergency response team is the immune system. It is an elite protection force, defending the body against disease. Different immune cells patrol the blood and another network of vessels called lymphatics, hunting down invading microbes such as viruses and bacteria. When the immune cells find these invaders, they blast them with special weapons.

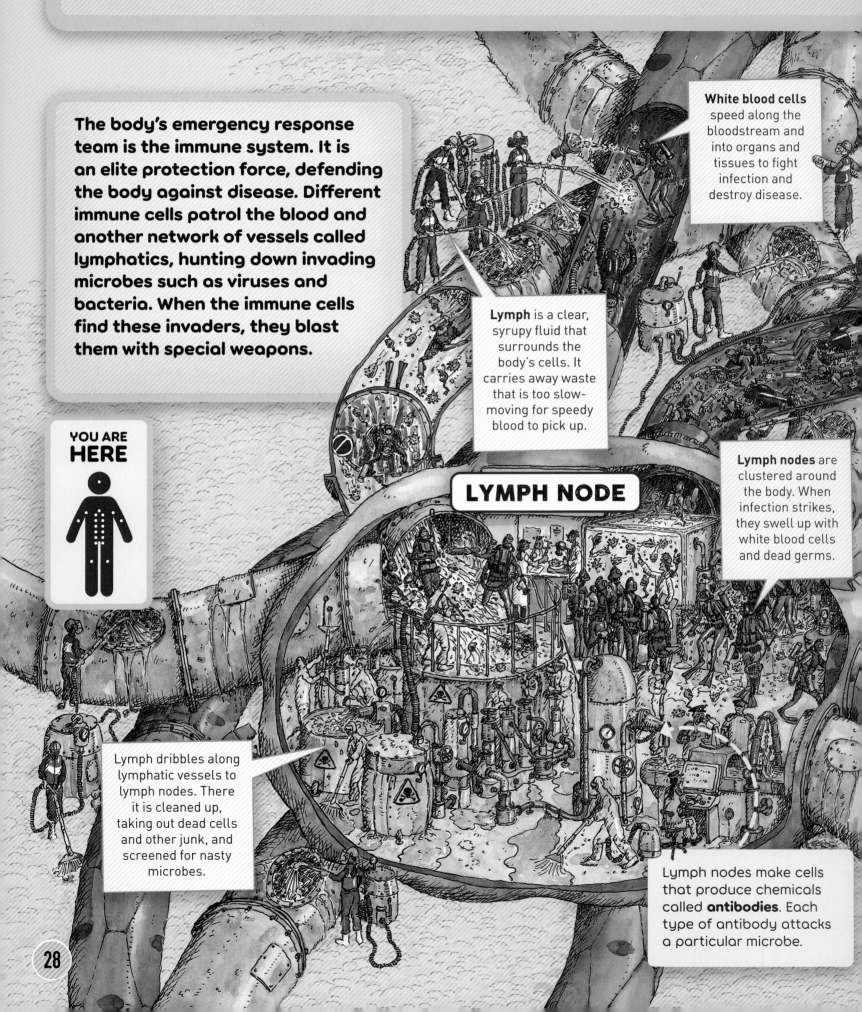

YOU ARE HERE

White blood cells speed along the bloodstream and into organs and tissues to fight infection and destroy disease.

Lymph is a clear, syrupy fluid that surrounds the body's cells. It carries away waste that is too slow-moving for speedy blood to pick up.

Lymph nodes are clustered around the body. When infection strikes, they swell up with white blood cells and dead germs.

LYMPH NODE

Lymph dribbles along lymphatic vessels to lymph nodes. There it is cleaned up, taking out dead cells and other junk, and screened for nasty microbes.

Lymph nodes make cells that produce chemicals called **antibodies**. Each type of antibody attacks a particular microbe.

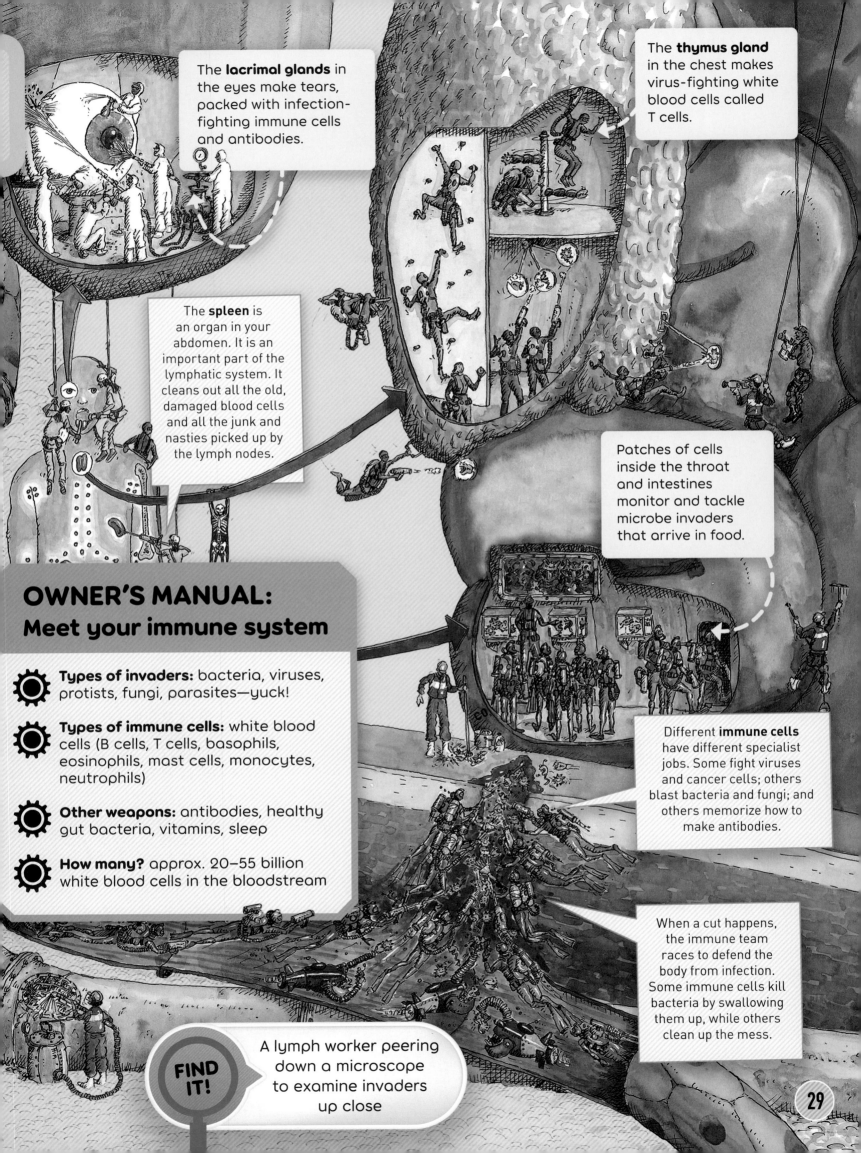

The **lacrimal glands** in the eyes make tears, packed with infection-fighting immune cells and antibodies.

The **thymus gland** in the chest makes virus-fighting white blood cells called T cells.

The **spleen** is an organ in your abdomen. It is an important part of the lymphatic system. It cleans out all the old, damaged blood cells and all the junk and nasties picked up by the lymph nodes.

Patches of cells inside the throat and intestines monitor and tackle microbe invaders that arrive in food.

OWNER'S MANUAL:
Meet your immune system

- ⚙ **Types of invaders:** bacteria, viruses, protists, fungi, parasites—yuck!

- ⚙ **Types of immune cells:** white blood cells (B cells, T cells, basophils, eosinophils, mast cells, monocytes, neutrophils)

- ⚙ **Other weapons:** antibodies, healthy gut bacteria, vitamins, sleep

- ⚙ **How many?** approx. 20–55 billion white blood cells in the bloodstream

Different **immune cells** have different specialist jobs. Some fight viruses and cancer cells; others blast bacteria and fungi; and others memorize how to make antibodies.

When a cut happens, the immune team races to defend the body from infection. Some immune cells kill bacteria by swallowing them up, while others clean up the mess.

FIND IT! A lymph worker peering down a microscope to examine invaders up close

29

BONES AND JOINTS

The human body is built around a tough inner framework—the skeleton, made up of bones. The skeleton supports the body's weight, protects vital organs, and provides a structure for the muscles to attach on to and pull on. Bones meet at joints, which are ingenious mechanisms that allow the body to bend.

Different kinds of joints fit the bill for different types of movements. For example, the knee and elbow only move up and down at a hinge joint. Shoulders and hips need to move around much more and have a ball-and-socket joint.

Hinge	Pivot	Ball-and-socket	Gliding	Saddle
knee, elbow	skull on spine	shoulder, hip	vertebrae, ankle, wrist	thumb

Surrounding the marrow is a layer of **spongy bone**. It looks like honeycomb and is holey but strong.

Bone has a hard outer layer called compact bone. It is full of bone cells called **osteocytes**, and these have their own blood supply.

Bones may seem dead, but they're very much alive! In the middle is a layer of gel-like stuff called **bone marrow**. It is busy making your blood cells.

A pocket of **synovial fluid** between the bones is like oil to keep the joint moving smoothly.

YOU ARE HERE

Bones need food. **Calcium** (from dairy products and some fruits, vegetables, and nuts) and **vitamin D** from sunlight keep them hard and strong.

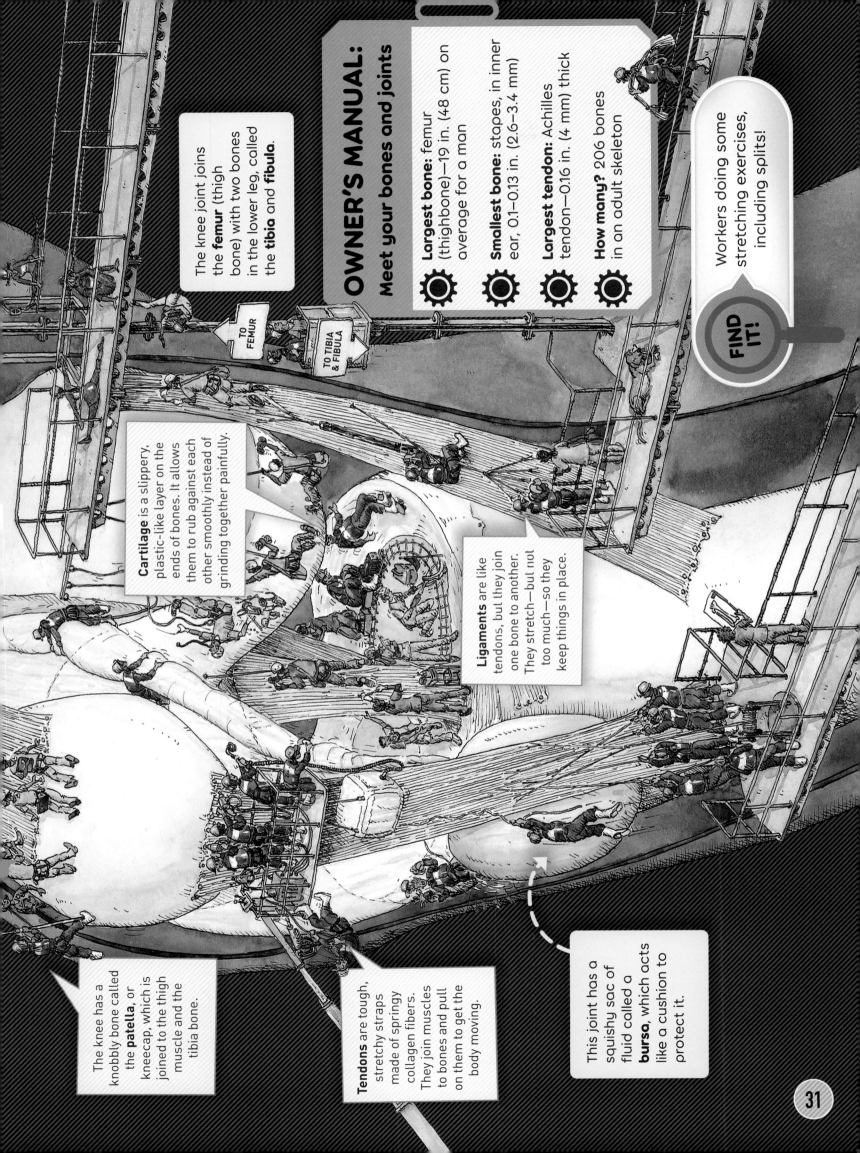

The knee joint joins the **femur** (thigh bone) with two bones in the lower leg, called the **tibia** and **fibula**.

TO FEMUR

TO TIBIA & FIBULA

OWNER'S MANUAL:
Meet your bones and joints

Largest bone: femur (thighbone)—19 in. (48 cm) on average for a man

Smallest bone: stapes, in inner ear, 0.1–0.13 in. (2.6–3.4 mm)

Largest tendon: Achilles tendon—0.16 in. (4 mm) thick

How many? 206 bones in an adult skeleton

FIND IT!

Workers doing some stretching exercises, including splits!

Cartilage is a slippery, plastic-like layer on the ends of bones. It allows them to rub against each other smoothly instead of grinding together painfully.

Ligaments are like tendons, but they join one bone to another. They stretch—but not too much—so they keep things in place.

The knee has a knobbly bone called the **patella**, or kneecap, which is joined to the thigh muscle and the tibia bone.

Tendons are tough, stretchy straps made of springy collagen fibers. They join muscles to bones and pull on them to get the body moving.

This joint has a squishy sac of fluid called a **bursa**, which acts like a cushion to protect it.

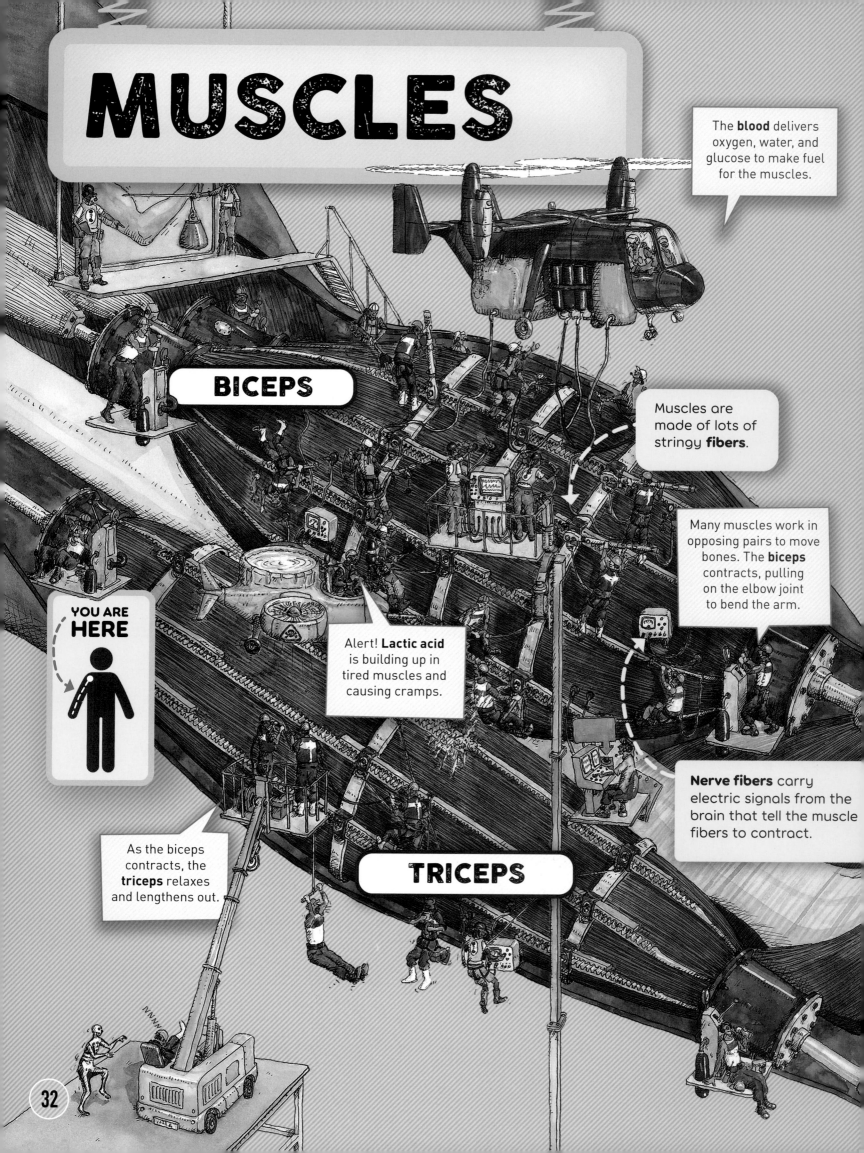

MUSCLES

The **blood** delivers oxygen, water, and glucose to make fuel for the muscles.

BICEPS

Muscles are made of lots of stringy **fibers**.

Many muscles work in opposing pairs to move bones. The **biceps** contracts, pulling on the elbow joint to bend the arm.

YOU ARE **HERE**

Alert! **Lactic acid** is building up in tired muscles and causing cramps.

Nerve fibers carry electric signals from the brain that tell the muscle fibers to contract.

As the biceps contracts, the **triceps** relaxes and lengthens out.

TRICEPS

When it's time to start moving, your muscles get to work. Some muscles are attached to your bones, and they move the body around, getting you walking and running as well as blinking and chewing. Other muscles drive your internal organs and coordinate your heartbeat. So come on, lazy bones—action, please!

OWNER'S MANUAL: Meet your muscles

- **Largest:** the gluteus maximus, in your bottom
- **Hardest working:** your heart muscles, because they never stop!
- **Fastest moving:** the muscles around your eyes
- **Smallest** the stapedius, in your ear

Calcium is vital for muscle control. Milk supplies on their way!

Muscles' stringy fibers are bundled together into cables. Zoom in really close and you'll see the fibers are made of cells as long as a 12 in. (30 cm) ruler but microscopically thin. And inside each one are bundles of even thinner stringy proteins called **filaments**.

When a fiber contracts, the filaments slide over one another like interlacing fingers. This shortens the fiber, pulling the ends of the muscle together and making it bulge.

Tough cords called **tendons** attach muscles to bones.

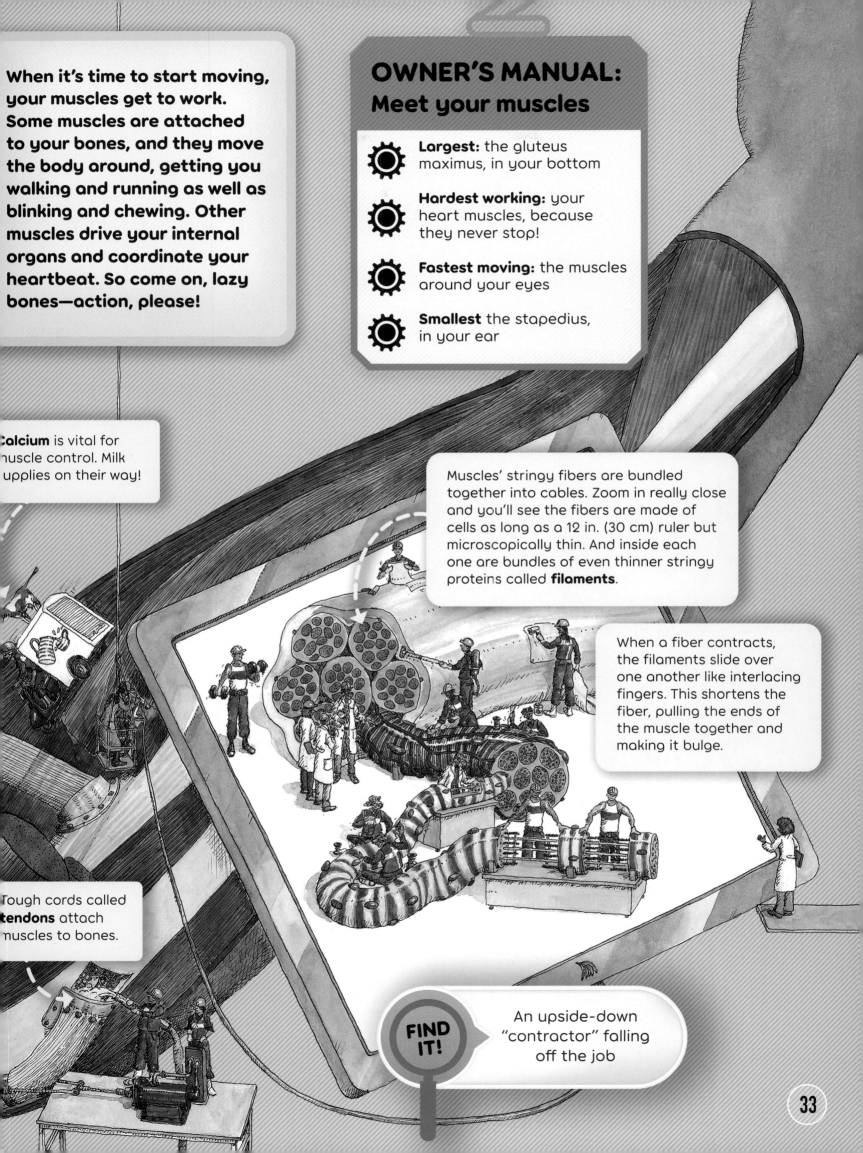

FIND IT! An upside-down "contractor" falling off the job

NERVOUS SYSTEM

The Human Body Factory tingles and twitches with electricity, which zaps through a network of nerves called the nervous system. This amazing communication superhighway links the brain with nerves, which carry signals all around the body. Through this network the brain controls muscles, operates organs, and monitors what's going on inside and outside the body.

Nerves are bundles of long, thin cells called **neurons**. They send signals as tiny jolts of electricity.

Motor nerves zap signals out from the brain to the muscles, telling them when and how to move.

Sensory nerves zap information from the senses to the brain. They register sight, smell, hearing, taste, and touch.

The **brain stem** is a junction between the spinal cord and the brain. It controls processes that keep the body going, such as heart rate and breathing.

The **spinal cord** is a thick bundle of nerves that runs all the way up the back. Signals zap both up and down it, to and from the brain.

Part of the nervous system called the **autonomic nervous system** controls your heartbeat and breathing, stomach and bladder action, and your blood pressure. It does all this automatically, without your having to think about it.

ON
OFF

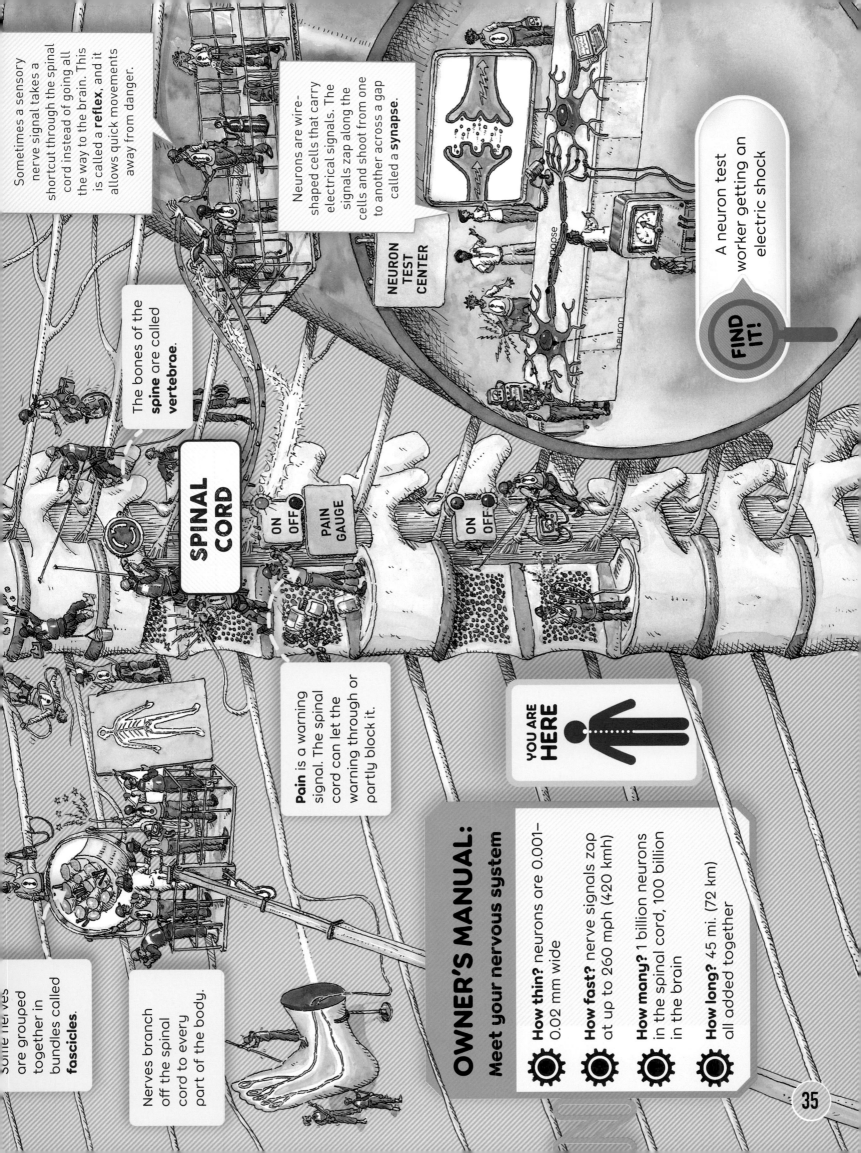

Sometimes a sensory nerve signal takes a shortcut through the spinal cord instead of going all the way to the brain. This is called a **reflex**, and it allows quick movements away from danger.

Neurons are wire-shaped cells that carry electrical signals. The signals zap along the cells and shoot from one to another across a gap called a **synapse**.

The bones of the **spine** are called **vertebrae.**

SPINAL CORD

ON OFF

PAIN GAUGE

ON OFF

NEURON TEST CENTER

FIND IT!

A neuron test worker getting an electric shock

Some nerves are grouped together in bundles called **fascicles.**

Nerves branch off the spinal cord to every part of the body.

Pain is a warning signal. The spinal cord can let the warning through or partly block it.

YOU ARE **HERE**

OWNER'S MANUAL:
Meet your nervous system

⚙ **How thin?** neurons are 0.001–0.02 mm wide

⚙ **How fast?** nerve signals zap at up to 260 mph (420 kmh)

⚙ **How many?** 1 billion neurons in the spinal cord, 100 billion in the brain

⚙ **How long?** 45 mi. (72 km) all added together

LUNGS

The lungs are a department with a lot of puff. Their job is to get vital oxygen into the body and force poisonous carbon dioxide out. Air enters and leaves the lungs through an intricate maze of branching tubes, which end in tiny bubbles where oxygen and carbon dioxide change places. Take a deep breath!

Intercostal muscles move the **rib cage** every time you breathe.

The **trachea** branches off into two big air pipes called **bronchi**, and then into lots of smaller tubes called **bronchioles**.

When you breathe in, your diaphragm muscle pulls downward. Intercostal muscles move your ribs up and outward. Air rushes in, and your lungs blow up like balloons.

As you breathe out, your diaphragm and intercostal muscles relax. The ribs close in and air pushes out of your lungs to leave through your nose or mouth.

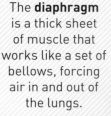

The **diaphragm** is a thick sheet of muscle that works like a set of bellows, forcing air in and out of the lungs.

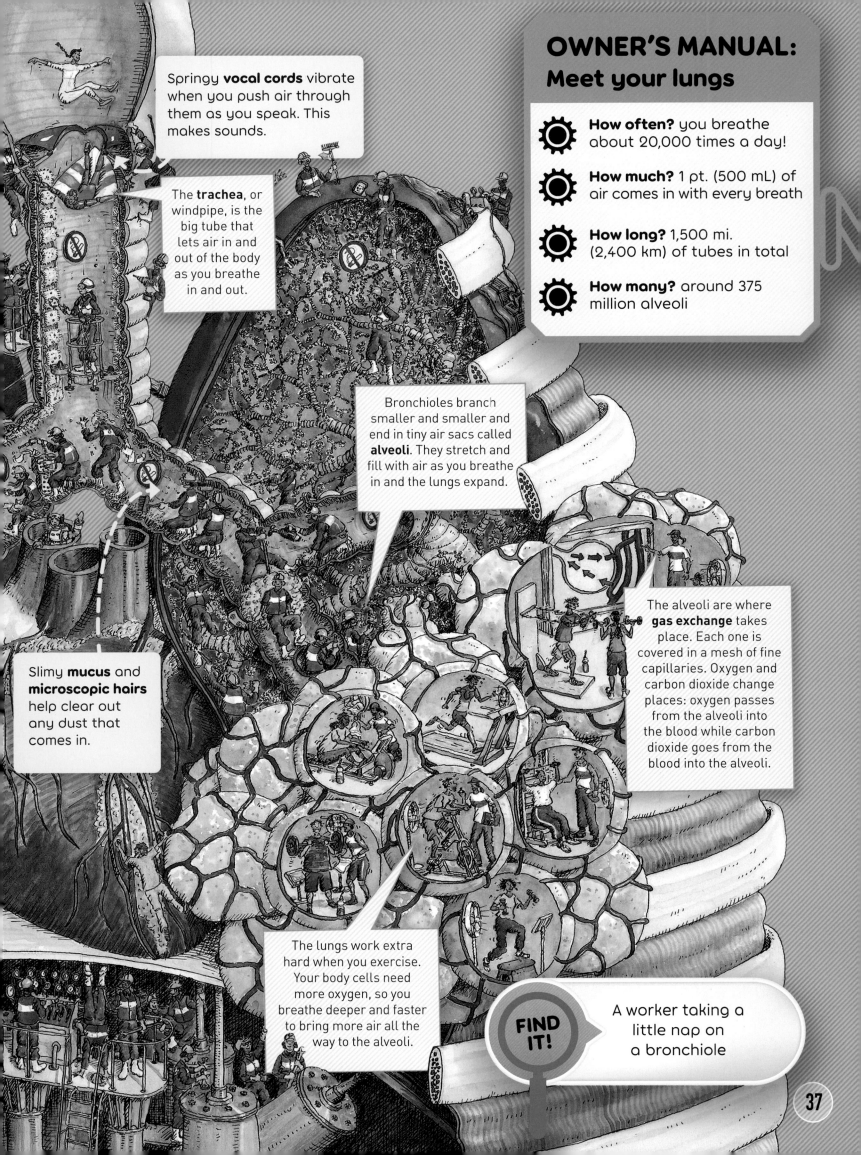

Springy **vocal cords** vibrate when you push air through them as you speak. This makes sounds.

The **trachea**, or windpipe, is the big tube that lets air in and out of the body as you breathe in and out.

OWNER'S MANUAL:
Meet your lungs

How often? you breathe about 20,000 times a day!

How much? 1 pt. (500 mL) of air comes in with every breath

How long? 1,500 mi. (2,400 km) of tubes in total

How many? around 375 million alveoli

Bronchioles branch smaller and smaller and end in tiny air sacs called **alveoli**. They stretch and fill with air as you breathe in and the lungs expand.

The alveoli are where **gas exchange** takes place. Each one is covered in a mesh of fine capillaries. Oxygen and carbon dioxide change places: oxygen passes from the alveoli into the blood while carbon dioxide goes from the blood into the alveoli.

Slimy **mucus** and **microscopic hairs** help clear out any dust that comes in.

The lungs work extra hard when you exercise. Your body cells need more oxygen, so you breathe deeper and faster to bring more air all the way to the alveoli.

FIND IT! A worker taking a little nap on a bronchiole

LIVER AND GALL BLADDER

EXIT (HEPATIC VEIN)

The **liver** sorts the good from the bad. Medicines are broken down and sent to work in the body. Toxins (poisons) are broken down. Some go into the bile; others go in the blood to the kidneys (see pages 40–41).

The liver's main jobs are done by chemical reaction units called **enzymes**.

The liver is amazingly good at repairing itself, but it's still better to steer clear of things that will harm it.

DELIVERIES

YOU ARE **HERE**

Bile is a bitter green liquid that the liver makes. It is stored in an organ called the **gall bladder** until it is needed to help with digestion.

FULL UP

HUNGRY

When the stomach releases its contents into the intestines, it's time for bile to get to work. It squirts into the intestines, where it dissolves fats in the food.

GALL BLADDER

The liver converts excess nitrogen in the blood into **urea**. This is filtered in the kidneys, and leaves the body in pee.

The liver stores some **vitamins and minerals** that arrive here in the blood. It makes others from the ingredients that arrive.

 How heavy? 3.3 lb. (1.5 kg)—the body's biggest internal organ

 How much bile? produces about 1 qt. (1 L) per day

 How much blood? contains about 10% of the blood in your body

 How many tasks? does 500 separate jobs

Urea makes pee smell, and the remains of old red blood cells make it yellow.

The liver converts carbohydrates in food into an **energy store** called glycogen. Later, when you need an energy boost, it converts glycogen into glucose, which is a fast fuel.

LIVER

UREA

BILE

The liver gets a lot of old, worn-out red blood cells from the spleen. It juices them up, recycles useful stuff, and sends some parts to the kidneys to go into pee.

The liver makes **cholesterol**, which is used to build cell walls and make hormones.

A hormone called **insulin**, made in the pancreas, controls the levels of glucose released from the liver into the blood.

Right in the middle of the Human Body Factory is the liver. It's like a big, busy kitchen processing lots of ingredients. The ingredients arrive in blood from the guts —goodies such as vitamins, sugars, iron, and fats, and bad stuff such as nasty toxins. The liver refines and stores nutrients, cleans the blood, and makes a juice called bile.

HEPATIC PORTAL VEIN

HEPATIC ARTERY

Blood comes into the liver from the stomach and intestines through the **hepatic portal vein**.

FIND IT! A worker nibbling on a glycogen energy bar

KIDNEYS AND BLADDER

YOU ARE **HERE**

The kidneys are a pair of waste treatment plants, where toxic garbage and excess water are removed from the blood. They clean the blood and produce a waste material—urine (pee)— which then flows to the bladder. The bladder is a stretchy bag that stores the urine until it is time to let it out of the body altogether.

Cleaned blood goes out along the **renal vein** to the heart, which sends it to the rest of the body.

The body gets rid of excess water in a few ways. The main one is **urination** (peeing).

Blood comes along the **renal artery** into the kidneys, ready for cleaning.

DIRTY BLOOD

CLEAN BLOOD

TO BLADDER

KIDNEY

In the nephrons, useful things such as sugars, salts, minerals, and proteins are removed and put back into the blood.

The **kidneys** filter all the body's blood at least 300 times every day. They also help balance the volume of fluids and salts in the body.

Each kidney has around a million tiny filtering units called **nephrons.** The nephrons filter the blood, working a little like a high-pressure coffee machine.

The nephrons squeeze out the watery parts of blood along with waste chemicals and some nutrients. These become a clear yellowy liquid—**urine** (pee).

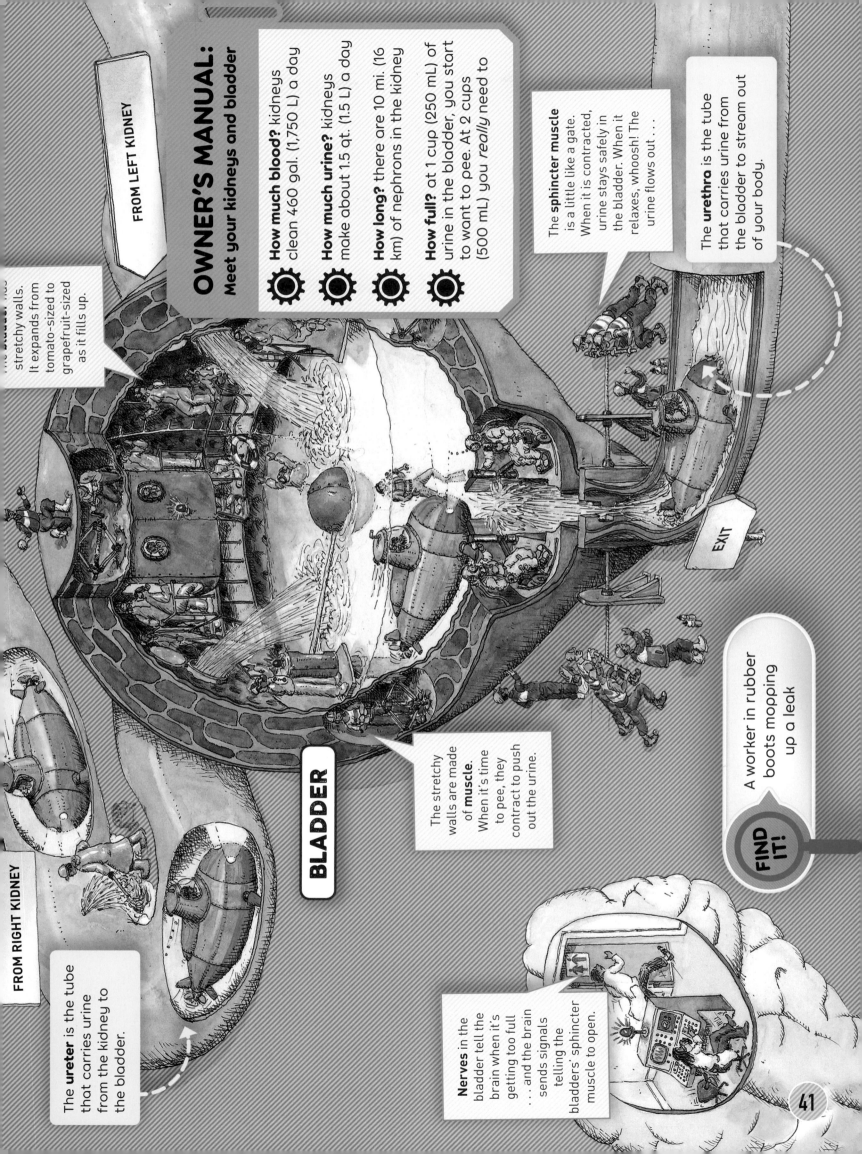

FROM LEFT KIDNEY

OWNER'S MANUAL:
Meet your kidneys and bladder

How much blood? kidneys clean 460 gal. (1,750 L) a day

How much urine? kidneys make about 1.5 qt. (1.5 L) a day

How long? there are 10 mi. (16 km) of nephrons in the kidney

How full? at 1 cup (250 mL) of urine in the bladder, you start to want to pee. At 2 cups (500 mL) you *really* need to

stretchy walls. It expands from tomato-sized to grapefruit-sized as it fills up.

The **sphincter muscle** is a little like a gate. When it is contracted, urine stays safely in the bladder. When it relaxes, whoosh! The urine flows out . . . .

The **urethra** is the tube that carries urine from the bladder to stream out of your body.

EXIT

BLADDER

The stretchy walls are made of **muscle**. When it's time to pee, they contract to push out the urine.

FROM RIGHT KIDNEY

The **ureter** is the tube that carries urine from the kidney to the bladder.

Nerves in the bladder tell the brain when it's getting too full . . . and the brain sends signals telling the bladders' sphincter muscle to open.

FIND IT!

A worker in rubber boots mopping up a leak

DIGESTION

Food comes into the body through the mouth, where digestion begins. It is swallowed down a pipe called the **esophagus** and arrives in the stomach.

In the **stomach**, the food is churned around in a mixture of stomach acid, enzymes, and useful bacteria. This partly digested food mush is called **chyme**.

A **sphincter muscle** works like a gate from the stomach to the small intestine.

The **small intestine** is where nutrients from the food pass across the lining into the blood. The villi increase the surface area of the lining so there is more space for this to happen.

Digestive juices contain **enzymes**, which work fast to break down the fats, proteins, and carbohydrates in food.

Chyme is very acidic. This is where gooey green **bile** comes in. It neutralizes the acid so that digestive juices can start to work. It also digests fats.

The lining of the small intestine is covered with millions of tiny finger-like bumps called **villi**.

Muscles in the intestine walls contract to push the food along.

The digestive system is the Human Body Factory's food processing plant. Food comes into the body, into the stomach, and along long, squishy tubes called intestines. In the intestines, nutrients are absorbed into the bloodstream, and then it's time to deal with the waste and get it out of the body. What goes in must come out—it's a stinky job!

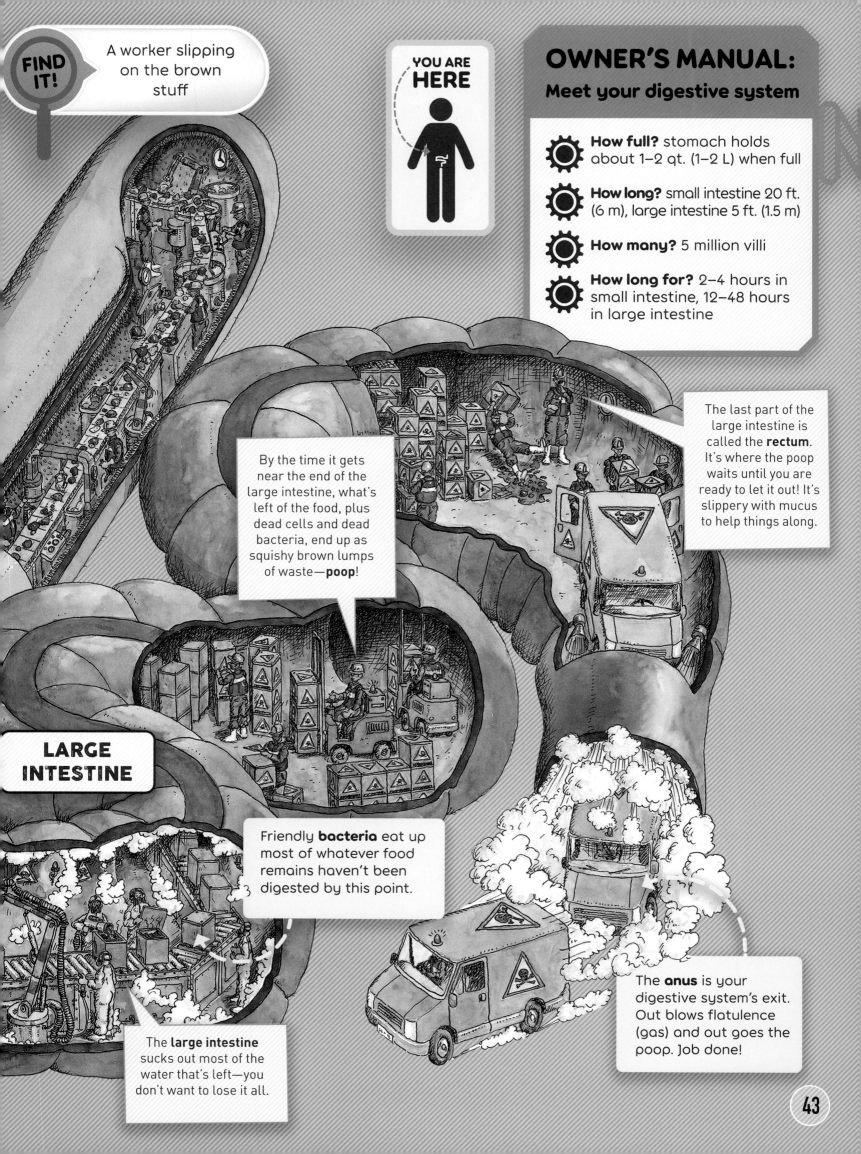

FIND IT! A worker slipping on the brown stuff

YOU ARE HERE

OWNER'S MANUAL:
Meet your digestive system

⚙ **How full?** stomach holds about 1–2 qt. (1–2 L) when full

⚙ **How long?** small intestine 20 ft. (6 m), large intestine 5 ft. (1.5 m)

⚙ **How many?** 5 million villi

⚙ **How long for?** 2–4 hours in small intestine, 12–48 hours in large intestine

The last part of the large intestine is called the **rectum**. It's where the poop waits until you are ready to let it out! It's slippery with mucus to help things along.

By the time it gets near the end of the large intestine, what's left of the food, plus dead cells and dead bacteria, end up as squishy brown lumps of waste—**poop**!

LARGE INTESTINE

Friendly **bacteria** eat up most of whatever food remains haven't been digested by this point.

The **large intestine** sucks out most of the water that's left—you don't want to lose it all.

The **anus** is your digestive system's exit. Out blows flatulence (gas) and out goes the poop. Job done!

REPRODUCTION

The **bladder** is not part of the reproductive system, but it releases its urine into the urethra in the penis.

The job of the reproductive system is to make new humans. It is different in males and females. Males have a penis and testes. Females have ovaries and a uterus (womb). Each system makes an unusual type of cell—sperm or eggs. One day, when a male sperm cell and a female egg cell meet, they will make a brand-new person.

The **seminal vesicles** make extra liquid to go into semen.

The **prostate gland** makes a milky, energy-filled liquid called **semen**, which powers sperm cells on their swim. It has muscles to pump the semen through the penis.

The **urethra** is the tube that carries urine as well as sperm out of the penis. It's important to keep the penis clean.

Each **testis** is held inside a sack called a **scrotum**. These help keep the testes at the right temperature—when it's cold, they pull them up to warm up, and when it's hot they lower them to cool off.

In an adult man, the testes are busy sperm factories. They churn out wriggly-tailed **sperm cells** and get them ready to swim off to meet an egg.

The **penis** dangles outside the body. When it's time for sperm to swim out, extra blood pumps into the penis and it gets stiff.

The **epididymis** is a twisty tube that stores sperm ready for their journey. When it's time for them to leave the body, they move into a tube called the **vas deferens**.

The testes also make **testosterone**. This hormone drives changes that happen in **puberty**, such as growing more body hair.

MAN

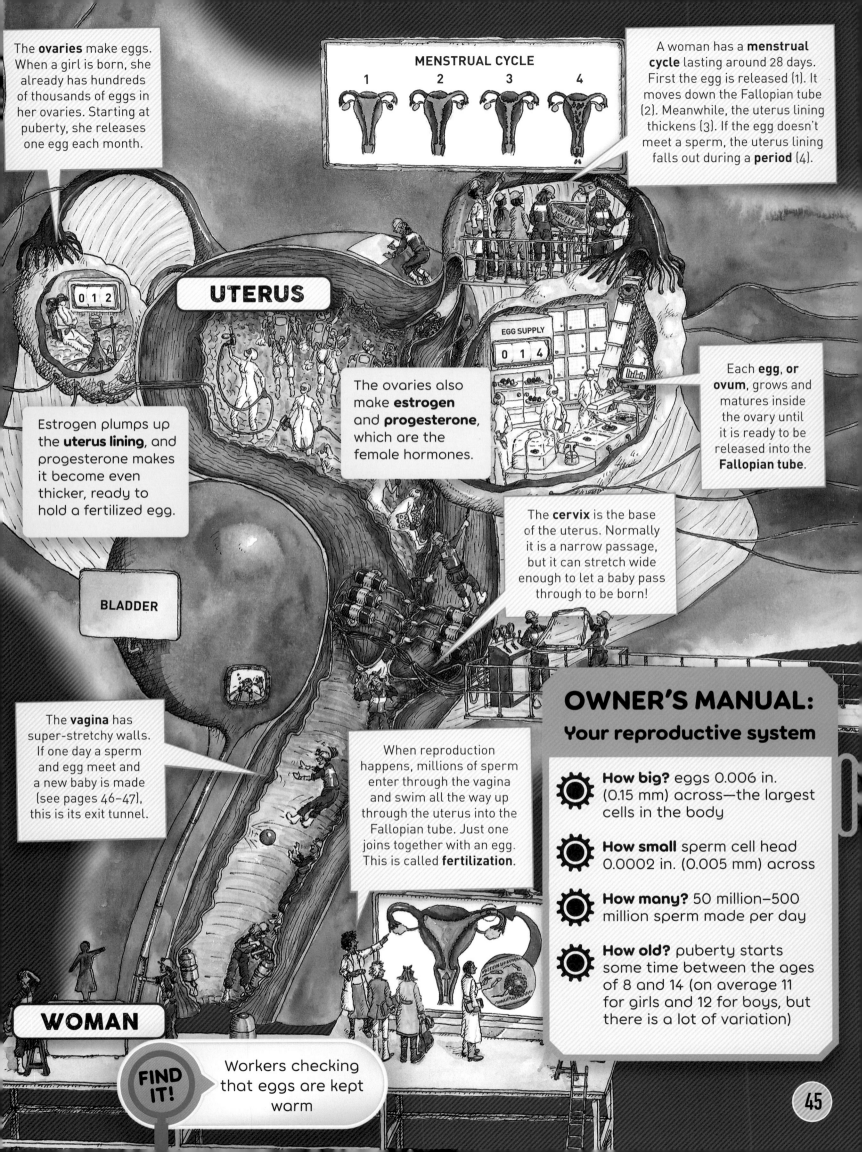

The **ovaries** make eggs. When a girl is born, she already has hundreds of thousands of eggs in her ovaries. Starting at puberty, she releases one egg each month.

MENSTRUAL CYCLE

1   2   3   4

A woman has a **menstrual cycle** lasting around 28 days. First the egg is released (1). It moves down the Fallopian tube (2). Meanwhile, the uterus lining thickens (3). If the egg doesn't meet a sperm, the uterus lining falls out during a **period** (4).

UTERUS

0 1 2

EGG SUPPLY

0 1 4

The ovaries also make **estrogen** and **progesterone**, which are the female hormones.

Each **egg, or ovum**, grows and matures inside the ovary until it is ready to be released into the **Fallopian tube**.

Estrogen plumps up the **uterus lining**, and progesterone makes it become even thicker, ready to hold a fertilized egg.

The **cervix** is the base of the uterus. Normally it is a narrow passage, but it can stretch wide enough to let a baby pass through to be born!

BLADDER

The **vagina** has super-stretchy walls. If one day a sperm and egg meet and a new baby is made (see pages 46–47), this is its exit tunnel.

When reproduction happens, millions of sperm enter through the vagina and swim all the way up through the uterus into the Fallopian tube. Just one joins together with an egg. This is called **fertilization**.

OWNER'S MANUAL:
Your reproductive system

⚙ **How big?** eggs 0.006 in. (0.15 mm) across—the largest cells in the body

⚙ **How small** sperm cell head 0.0002 in. (0.005 mm) across

⚙ **How many?** 50 million–500 million sperm made per day

⚙ **How old?** puberty starts some time between the ages of 8 and 14 (on average 11 for girls and 12 for boys, but there is a lot of variation)

WOMAN

FIND IT! Workers checking that eggs are kept warm

PREGNANCY

Fertilization happens when a **sperm cell** meets an **egg cell**. Millions of swimming sperm may reach the egg, but only one gets through the egg wall to fertilize it.

FROM OVARY

DAY 1

DAY 3

DAY 4

UTERUS

The sperm and egg fuse together to form a single cell. In 24 hours, this divides in two. It keeps dividing until it is a **ball of many cells**.

Making a teeny-weeny new model human is one of the most incredible things the Human Body Factory can do. The female body contains all the equipment needed to build a baby. Building starts when a sperm cell enters the body and meets an egg cell. The process is called pregnancy and takes about 40 weeks from fertilization to birth.

The ball of cells grows a yolk sac, amniotic sac, and placenta, as well as the **embryo**, which is the developing baby.

Implantation happens—the ball of cells burrows into the uterus wall with its nice, plump lining and settles in place.

placenta

umbilical cord

mother's blood—nutrients

baby's blood

waste

6 WEEKS

The **placenta** lets oxygen and nutrients pass from the mother's blood to the baby's, and it takes waste in the other direction. The **umbilical cord** links the baby to the placenta.

The **amniotic sac** is a strong, fluid-filled bag that protects the baby from bumps.

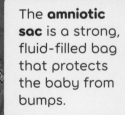

At six weeks, the embryo already has a brain and a heart. Its limbs are just buds, its hands and feet are webbed, and it has a tail!

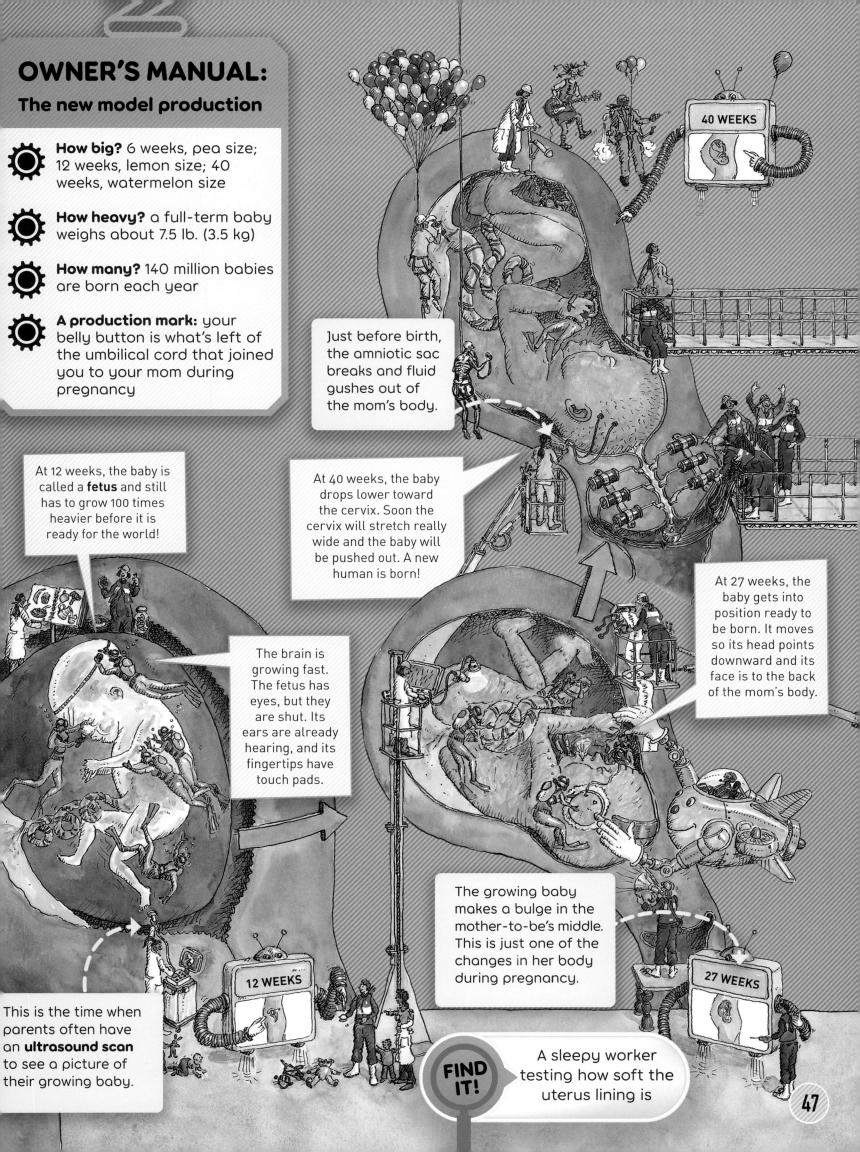

OWNER'S MANUAL:
The new model production

⚙ **How big?** 6 weeks, pea size; 12 weeks, lemon size; 40 weeks, watermelon size

⚙ **How heavy?** a full-term baby weighs about 7.5 lb. (3.5 kg)

⚙ **How many?** 140 million babies are born each year

⚙ **A production mark:** your belly button is what's left of the umbilical cord that joined you to your mom during pregnancy

Just before birth, the amniotic sac breaks and fluid gushes out of the mom's body.

At 12 weeks, the baby is called a **fetus** and still has to grow 100 times heavier before it is ready for the world!

At 40 weeks, the baby drops lower toward the cervix. Soon the cervix will stretch really wide and the baby will be pushed out. A new human is born!

The brain is growing fast. The fetus has eyes, but they are shut. Its ears are already hearing, and its fingertips have touch pads.

At 27 weeks, the baby gets into position ready to be born. It moves so its head points downward and its face is to the back of the mom's body.

The growing baby makes a bulge in the mother-to-be's middle. This is just one of the changes in her body during pregnancy.

This is the time when parents often have an **ultrasound scan** to see a picture of their growing baby.

FIND IT! A sleepy worker testing how soft the uterus lining is

40 WEEKS

12 WEEKS

27 WEEKS

AMAZING BODY FACTS

From the moment you leave your mother's womb, pop out into the world, and take your first breath, your body is working hard to keep you up and running. It does a million marvelous things for you—like reading this book, for instance! Life is full of mind-blowing surprising facts.

The ridges on your fingertips can feel bumps about 100 times smaller than anything you can see.

The human body contains enough:
Carbon to make about 900 pencils
Nitrogen to fill a soda can
Phosphorus to make 2,000 matches
Iron for a standard nail
Sulfur to de-flea a dog
Fat to make 7 bars of soap
Water to fill 11 gallon-sized milk jugs

Your skin cells completely regrow in a month. Dead skin cells fall off (and make up most of the dust in your house—eew)!

HUMAN BODY FACT FILE (ADULTS)

Number of bones: 206

Average body temperature: 98.6°F (37°C)

Average pulse rate: 60–90 beats per minute; athletes as low as 40 bpm

Number of muscles: approx. 650

Number of brain cells: more than 86 billion neurons

Number of brain cells lost every day: 85,000

Total dead skin shed in a lifetime: approx. 77 lb. (35 kg)

Number of cell types: approx. 220

Average total blood volume: 10.5 pt. (5 L)

Total surface area of skin: approx. 20 sq. ft. (1.86 m^2)

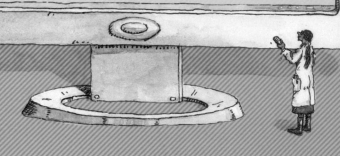

If all the blood vessels in your body were joined together end-to-end, they would stretch around the world almost two and a half times!

Your brain is one of the heaviest organs, around 3 lb. (1.4 kg). It's already 2.4 lb. (1.1 kg)—and almost fully grown—when you're three years old.

Your brain runs on 12 watts of power—less than the light in a refrigerator uses! But just think of all the work that power does.

Your senses are amazing . . .

You can feel a bee's wing gently brushing your cheek.

Your body creates and destroys around 2.5 million red blood cells every second!

You might have 105,000 dreams in your lifetime.

You can taste 1 teaspoon of sugar in 2 gal. (8 L) of water.

You can hear a watch ticking 20 ft. (6 m) away.

You can smell a single drop of perfume in a six-bedroom apartment.

GLOSSARY

Adrenal gland A gland that reacts to stress by making hormones that make the heart race and get the body ready for action. One sits on top of each kidney.

Antibodies Proteins made by white blood cells as part of the body's immune system, to attack germs and help fight infection

Bacteria Microscopic single-celled organisms, also called microbes or germs. Some cause infection in the body, while others are "friendly" bacteria that live in the intestines and on the skin.

Cardiovascular system The system that transports blood around the body, powered by the heart

Cartilage Tough but flexible material that protects the ends of bones at joints. It also gives structure to body parts such as the nose, outer ear, and tubes in the lungs and throat.

Cell The body's building block; cells make all the body's tissues and organs, and do all its basic jobs.

Cerebral cortex The "wrinkly" outer part of the cerebrum (brain)

Cholesterol A chemical made in the liver from fats in the food we eat that is used to build cell walls. Too much cholesterol in the blood can damage blood vessels and lead to heart problems.

Chyme A gloopy fluid made up of squished-up half-digested food, stomach acids, and enzymes. It is what food has become by the time it leaves the stomach and passes to the small intestine.

Coronary Anything to do with the arteries that supply the heart with blood

Dairy products Milk and foods that are made from milk, such as butter and cheese.

Dentine The hard material underneath a tooth's outer coating of enamel

Digestive system The system of tubes that breaks down food and absorbs it into the body.

Embryo The name for a developing baby up to the eighth week of pregnancy

Enamel The hard and glossy coating on a tooth

Endocrine system The system that controls what goes on inside the body using chemical messengers called hormones

Enzyme A protein that speeds up chemical reactions in the body

Epiglottis A flap of cartilage at the back of the throat that stops food and liquid from getting into the lungs

Fetus A developing baby from the eighth week of pregnancy until birth

Glucose A sugar that is the body's main energy source.

Gonads The sex organs (male or female)

Hepatic Anything to do with the liver

Hormone A chemical messenger that carries a signal from one cell to another. Hormones are released by glands and cells.

Immune system The defense system that protects the body from infection

Intercostal muscles Muscles between the ribs that help with breathing

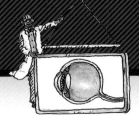
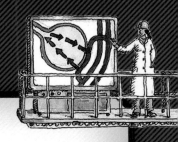

Lactic acid A mildly toxic waste product made by muscles during heavy exercise (when not enough oxygen is getting to the muscles)

Lobe A rounded body part that often forms a section of a large organ such as the brain, liver, or lungs

Lymph A clear fluid that surrounds all body cells

Lymphatic system The body system that drains and transports lymph and works with the immune system to fight infection

Meninges Protective layers surrounding the brain and spinal cord

Mucus A slimy bodily fluid produced by the linings or coverings of organs

Musculoskeletal system The skeleton and muscles, the load-bearing system that supports the body and pulls on it to move it around

Nervous system The network of nerve cells and fibers that sends information around the body as electrical pulses.

Neuron A single nerve cell

Nutrients Vital chemicals we get from food, needed for the body's smooth running and growth

Osteocyte A bone-making cell

Proteins A group of essential body chemicals that are used to build new tissues such as muscle fibers, hair, and nails. Antibodies and enzymes are also proteins.

Pulmonary Anything to do with the lungs

Renal Anything to do with the kidneys

Reproductive system The body system that makes sex cells (sperm in males and eggs in females) and takes charge of making new humans

Respiratory system The system in charge of breathing air—bringing fresh oxygen into the body and releasing waste carbon dioxide

Sinus A cave-like opening in a bone that can often fill with fluid

Sphincter A ring of muscle controlling an opening in the body—for example, the anus or the bladder's outlet

Synapse A gap between neurons that allows one neuron to pass on an electrical or chemical signal to another neuron

Tissue A group of the same or similar type of cells that work together to carry out a task

Urea A waste product from the breakdown of proteins in the body. It is removed from the body in urine (pee).

Urinary system The system that filters waste and excess water from the blood and releases it from the body as urine (pee)

Viruses Tiny infectious germs, usually much smaller than bacteria, that multiply inside cells

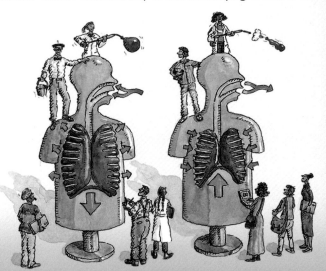

QUIZ

THE BRAIN

1. What is the largest part of the brain?
2. What bony case protects the brain?
3. Which part of the brain makes and stores memories?
4. Which part of the brain controls common movements without your really thinking about them?

EYES

1. What is the colored part of the eye called?
2. What are the light-sensing cells called?
3. What is the light-sensing lining of the eye called?
4. What is the big nerve in each eye called?

EARS

1. What's the name of the fleshy part of the outer ear?
2. What are the three tiny bones in the middle ear called?
3. What sticky substance traps dust in the ear canal?
4. What separates the outer ear from the middle ear?

NOSE

1. What do nostril hairs do?
2. What is the name of the bone in your nose?
3. What is another name for mucus in the nose?
4. What does the olfactory bulb do?

MOUTH

1. How many teeth does the human body have?
2. What are the five main taste types?
3. What is the proper name for spit?
4. What is the hard outer coating of the tooth called?

HORMONES

1. Which gland is the hormone control center?
2. How do hormones travel around the body?
3. Which gland sets the body clock?
4. Where would you find your thyroid gland?

SKIN, HAIR, AND NAILS

1. What are the three layers of the skin called?
2. Sweat pours out of little holes in the skin called what?
3. What grows out of a follicle?
4. Where is the thickest skin on the body?

HEART

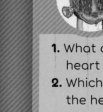

1. What are the upper and lower chambers of the heart called?
2. Which big artery takes oxygenated blood from the heart to the body?
3. Blood flows through the heart in a set one-way pattern. True or false?
4. The pulmonary artery takes blood from the heart to . . . where?

BLOOD

1. Which blood vessels have thick, strong walls and take blood away from the heart?
2. Which blood vessels have thinner walls and take blood back to the heart?
3. Which blood cells are red and doughnut shaped?
4. What are the tiny blood vessels called?

IMMUNE SYSTEM

1. Name any of the invaders the immune system fights.
2. Where are the lacrimal glands found?
3. Which gland makes white blood cells called T cells?
4. What can happen to your lymph nodes if you get an infection?

BONES AND JOINTS

1. Name two things that keep bones hard and strong.
2. Where do bones meet?
3. What is another name for the knobbly bone called the patella?
4. How many bones does an adult human have?

MUSCLES

1. What are the two big muscles in the upper arm called?
2. Where is your largest muscle, the gluteus maximus?
3. What happens when lactic acid builds up in your muscles?
4. Which muscles move the fastest?

NERVOUS SYSTEM

1. What is the bundle of nerves that runs all the way down your back called?
2. What are nerve cells called?
3. What are the bones of the spine called?
4. Which nerves carry messages telling your muscles to move?

LUNGS

1. What is another name for the trachea?
2. The air pipes in the lungs end in tiny bubble-like air sacs called what?
3. What two things help clear out any dust that comes into your lungs?
4. Do the lungs work harder when you exercise, or not as hard?

LIVER AND GALL BLADDER

1. How heavy is the liver?
2. The liver breaks down and gets rid of poisons. True or false?
3. What is the name of the bitter green liquid the liver makes?
4. What makes pee yellow?

KIDNEYS AND BLADDER

1. How many tiny filtering units does each kidney have: 10,000, 1 million, or 10 million?
2. What waste material do the kidneys make?
3. Is the blood clean or dirty when it leaves the kidneys?
4. Are the bladder walls stiff or stretchy?

DIGESTION

1. What are the two parts of the intestine called?
2. What is the name for the tiny finger-like bumps on the inside of the intestine wall?
3. How does food move along inside the intestines?
4. Which part of the intestines is where poop waits to come out?

REPRODUCTION

1. What are the two main reproductive organs in males?
2. What special cells do the testes make?
3. What are the two main reproductive organs in females?
4. What is another name for an ovum cell?

QUIZ ANSWERS

The brain
1. the cerebrum
2. the skull
3. the hippocampus
4. the cerebellum

Eyes
1. the iris
2. rods and cones
3. the retina
4. the optic nerve

Ears
1. pinna
2. malleus, incus, and stapes
3. wax
4. eardrum

Nose
1. stop dust, soot, pollen, and flies from getting inside your nose
2. the bridge
3. snot
4. zaps signals from smell detectors to the brain

Mouth
1. 32
2. sweet, salty, sour, bitter, umami (savory)
3. saliva
4. enamel

Hormones
1. the pituitary gland
2. in the bloodstream
3. the pineal gland
4. in your neck

Skin, hair, and nails
1. epidermis, dermis, and fat layer
2. pores
3. hair
4. the soles of the feet

Heart
1. atria and ventricles
2. the aorta
3. true
4. the lungs

Blood
1. arteries
2. veins
3. red blood cells
4. capillaries

Immune system
1. bacteria, viruses, fungi, cancer cells
2. in the eyes
3. the thymus gland
4. they swell up

Bones and joints
1. calcium and vitamin D
2. at joints
3. kneecap
4. 206

Muscles
1. biceps and triceps
2. in your bottom
3. you get a cramp
4. eye muscles

Nervous system
1. the spinal cord
2. neurons
3. vertebrae
4. motor nerves

Lungs
1. windpipe
2. alveoli
3. mucus and microscopic hairs
4. harder

Liver and gall bladder
1. 3.3 lb. (1.5 kg)
2. true
3. bile
4. the remains of old red blood cells

Kidneys and bladder
1. 1 million
2. urine (pee)
3. clean
4. stretchy

Digestion
1. small intestine and large intestine
2. villi
3. muscles squeeze it along
4. rectum

Reproduction
1. the penis and testes
2. sperm
3. the ovaries and uterus (womb)
4. an egg

FIND IT!

Did you find all the workers mentioned in the 'Find it!' magnifying glasses? Here they all are:

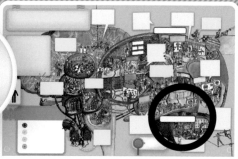

Pages 10–11 The Brain

Pages 12–13 Eyes

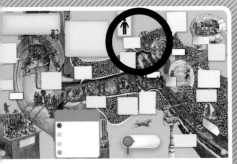
Pages 14–15 Ears

Pages 16–17 Nose

Pages 18–19 Mouth

Pages 20–21 Hormones

Pages 22–23 Skin, Hair, and Nails

Pages 24–25 Heart

Pages 26–27 Blood

Pages 28–29 Immune System

Pages 30–31 Bones and Joints

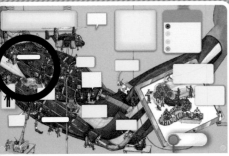
Pages 32–33 Muscles

Pages 34–35 Nervous System

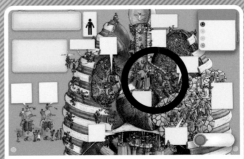
Pages 36–37 Lungs

Pages 38–39 Liver and Gall Bladder

Pages 40–41 Kidneys and Bladder

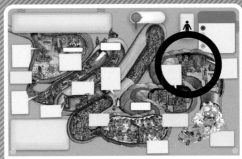
Pages 42–43 Digestion

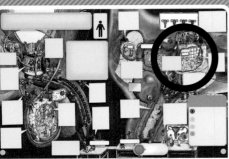
Pages 44–45 Reproduction

Pages 46–47 Pregnancy

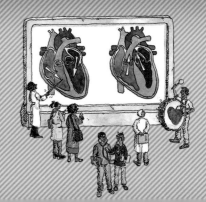

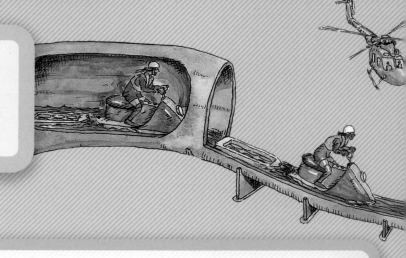

INDEX

antibodies 28, 29, 50, 51
arteries 24, 26, 27, 40, 50
babies 45, 46–47
bacteria 16, 19, 23, 27, 29, 42, 43, 50
balance 11, 15
bladder 9, 39, 40–41, 44
blood 7, 9, 20, 21, 23, 24, 25, 26–27, 28, 30, 32, 37, 38, 39, 40, 42, 44, 46
blood vessels 10, 18, 23, 25, 26, 27, 49
bones 7, 14, 15, 16, 17, 18, 30–31, 33, 35, 48,
brain 6, 9, 10–11, 13, 14, 15, 17, 19, 21, 22, 32, 34, 35, 47, 48, 49
breathing 8, 36–37
carbon dioxide 8, 9, 27, 36, 37
cardiovascular system 9, 24–25
cartilage 16, 31, 50
cells 8, 9, 10, 13, 19, 20, 21, 22, 24, 26, 27, 28, 29, 30, 33, 34, 35, 37, 39, 44, 45, 46, 48, 49, 50
digestive system 9, 18, 42–43, 50
ears 14–15
endocrine system 8, 20–21, 50

energy 10, 20, 39,
exercise 20, 26, 37,
eyes 12–13, 29, 47
fat 22, 26, 38, 42,
gall bladder 38
glands 19, 20, 21, 22, 23, 29, 44
glucose 32, 39, 50
hairs 8, 14, 15, 16, 22–23, 37, 44
hearing 11, 14–15, 35, 47
heart 9, 24–25, 26, 46
hormones 8, 20–21, 39, 44, 45, 50
immune system 8, 28–29, 50
intestines 9, 38, 42, 43
kidneys 9, 40–41
ligaments 31
liver 9, 38–39,
lungs 8, 9, 24, 36–37
lymph 28, 51
menstrual cycle 45
mouth 9, 18–19, 42
mucus 16, 37, 43, 51
muscles 9, 13, 19, 23, 24, 27, 30, 32–33, 34, 36, 41, 42, 43, 48
nails 8, 22
nerves 10, 13, 14, 15, 16, 17, 18, 19, 23, 32, 34–35, 41,
nervous system 9, 34–35, 51
neurons 10, 34, 35, 51

nose 16–17,
nutrients 24, 26, 27, 39, 40, 42, 46, 51
organs 6, 22, 30, 38
ovaries 44, 45
oxygen 8, 10, 24, 25, 26, 27, 32, 36, 37, 46
penis 44
pregnancy 46–47
puberty 44, 45
reproduction 9, 44–45
saliva 19
senses 11, 13, 16, 19, 22, 34, 49
skeleton 7, 9, 30, 31
skin 7, 8, 22–23, 48
sleep 21
smell 16–17, 19, 49
speech 11, 37
stomach 9, 42
taste 16, 19, 49
teeth 18, 19
tendons 31, 33
touch 22
urinary system 9, 40–41, 51
urine (pee) 40, 41, 44
vagina 45
veins 24, 26, 27, 39, 41,
viruses 27, 28, 29, 51
waste 9, 24, 26, 27, 28, 40, 42, 43, 46